THIS BOOK
BELONGS TO:

Susan Bell

The Legend of
Pocahontas

CHILDREN'S CLASSICS

This unique series of Children's Classics™ features accessible and highly readable texts paired with the work of talented and brilliant illustrators of bygone days to create fine editions for today's parents and children to rediscover and treasure. Besides being a handsome addition to any home library, this series features genuine bonded-leather spines stamped in gold, full-color illustrations, and high-quality acid-free paper that will enable these books to be passed from one generation to the next.

Adventures of Huckleberry Finn
The Adventures of Tom Sawyer
Aesop's Fables
Alice's Adventures in Wonderland
Andersen's Fairy Tales
Anne of Avonlea
Anne of Green Gables
At the Back of the North Wind
Black Beauty
The Call of the Wild
A Child's Book of Country Stories
A Child's Book of Stories
A Child's Book of Stories from Many
    Lands
A Child's Christmas
A Christmas Carol and Other
    Christmas Stories
Cinderella and Other Classic Italian
    Fairy Tales
The Complete Mother Goose
Goldilocks and the Three Bears and
    Other Classic English Fairy Tales
Great Dog Stories
Grimm's Fairy Tales
Hans Brinker *or* The Silver Skates
Heidi
The Hound of the Baskervilles
Joan of Arc

The Jungle Book
Just So Stories
Kidnapped
King Arthur and His Knights
The Legend of Pocahontas
A Little Child's Book of Stories
Little Men
A Little Princess
Little Women
Peter Pan
Pollyanna
The Prince and the Pauper
Rebecca of Sunnybrook Farm
Robin Hood
Robinson Crusoe
The Secret Garden
The Sleeping Beauty and Other
    Classic French Fairy Tales
The Swiss Family Robinson
Tales from Shakespeare
Tales of Pirates and Buccaneers
Through the Looking Glass and
    What Alice Found There
Treasure Island
A Very Little Child's Book of Stories
The Wind in the Willows
The Wonderful Wizard of Oz

The Legend of Pocahontas

Originally titled *The Princess Pocahontas*

By VIRGINIA WATSON

Retold by KARLA DOUGHERTY

Illustrated by GEORGE WHARTON EDWARDS

CHILDREN' CLASSICS
New York • Avenel

Originally titled *The Princess Pocahontas*

Text copyright 1995 by Random House Value Publishing, Inc.
All rights reserved.

This edition is published by Children's Classics, an imprint
and trademark of Random House Value Publishing, Inc.,
40 Engelhard Avenue, Avenel, New Jersey 07001.

Printed and bound in the United States of America

Library of Congress Cataloging-in-Publication Data

Dougherty, Karla.
 The legend of Pocahontas : originally titled The Princess Pocahontas /
by Virginia Watson : retold by Karla Dougherty ; illustrated by George
Wharton Edwards.
  p.   cm.
  ISBN 0–517–12225–1
  1. Pocahontas, d. 1617—Juvenile literature.   2. Powhatan Indians—
Biography—Juvenile literature.   3. Powhatan Indians—Social life and
customs—Juvenile literature.   4. Jamestown (Va.)—History—Juvenile
literature.   I. Edwards, George Wharton, 1859–1950.   II. Watson,
Virginia, b. 1872. Princess Pocahontas.   III. Title.
E99.P85P5727   1995
975.5′01′092—dc20
 [B]   94–40657
                                                                    CIP
                                                                     AC

Cover illustration copyright © by Shannon Stirnweis

Cover design by Mary Helen Fink
Production supervision by Roméo Enriquez
Editorial supervision by Claire Booss

10   9   8   7   6   5   4   3   2   1

ILLUSTRATIONS IN COLOR

PREFACE TO THIS ILLUSTRATED EDITION

George Wharton Edwards, who created these vivid paintings and drawings, was an American artist whose work appeared in many magazines and books in the first quarter of the twentieth century.

Edwards studied painting in Antwerp and Paris, and later, when traveling through Europe, was so impressed by the scenery, that he painted many of the places that he visited. Subsequently, however, he returned to the United States and concentrated on illustration.

The Legend of Pocahontas is, perhaps, the most American of tales that he could have chosen to illustrate—the story of the Native American princess whose loyalty to John Smith and whose concern for the Virginia colonists moved her to sacrifice and suffer so that they might survive and prosper.

Edwards has captured beautifully the color and drama of this extraordinary story and provided it with another dimension.

CLAIRE BOOSS
Series Editor

1995

INTRODUCTION

"Suddenly, with a quick leap, Pocahontas flung herself across Smith's body, took his head in her arms, and laid her own head down against his. The tomahawk had stopped but a feather's breadth from her black hair, so close that the Indian who held it could scarcely breathe for fear it might have injured the daughter of Chief Powhatan." This image of Pocahontas, with her long, dark braids, kneeling next to Captain John Smith just as a brave is about to lower an axe, is one that is indelibly imprinted in our minds, as much a part of schoolroom memories as the multiplication tables or learning to read. Indeed, people everywhere remember Pocahontas, the quintessential Indian princess, as the young heroine who, with one courageous act, saved the life of a handsome English army officer—and the future of the Virginia colony.

But there is much more to the Pocahontas legend than this one classic scene. In this book, fact and fiction, history and legend blend to re-create the life and the personality of this famous Native American. There are the childish pranks played by an impish girl whose real name is Matoaka, which means mischievous and full of joy. There is her daily life, free and spirited, as she roams the forest before the white man comes.

Her father is the powerful Chief Powhatan, a strong leader who rules thirty Algonquin tribes in what later will be called the Chesapeake Bay area. She is her father's favorite child and always gets her way—whether it is the opportunity to visit the strange white men who have begun to settle on the island they call Jamestown or the "adoption" of Captain John Smith into her tribe to save his life.

The story of Pocahontas includes love and high adventure, and betrayal by Indian and white friends alike. Although she is deeply in love with Captain John Smith, when she is told that he is dead, she marries Sir John Rolfe, another white settler. She embraces his ways and was the first Indian to become a Christian. Baptized Rebecca, she visits England and is presented to Queen Anne, who later called Lady Rebecca "one of the gentlest ladies England has ever welcomed."

And there is even an episode in which Pocahontas is kidnapped —and is forced to choose between a promise she made to Captain John Smith and a safe, long life among her own people.

These are some of the facets of the life of Pocahontas, a young woman who shows unbelievable courage when strangers first appear on her shores. Others might run and hide deeper in the forest, but Pocahontas bravely goes to meet the new world. She listens, she learns, and, ultimately, she makes a decision that could alienate her from her people, her very roots. And those roots were very deep.

In the days of Pocahontas, the land was very different than it is today. North America was territory practically untouched by foreign influence. It was the land of the Native Americans, from the Hopi in the west to the Algonquins in the east. Those people, including the Powhatans, the tribe of Pocahontas, respected and revered the land. Those people were not "primitive"—as the white men who sailed to the new world claimed. Although they did not have gunpowder or ships or written languages, they had a real knowledge of their land. They knew when to plant and when to harvest. They knew when and where to hunt and to fish.

They had, and have, a different culture, which was reflected in their dances, their painted adornment, their very survival.

When the first white men appeared in the bay, sailing across the water on what seemed to be miraculous white wings, it must have been an astonishing sight to those Native Americans, an image as terrifying as it was mesmerizing. And the culture they brought with them was so alien. From the elaborate clothing the men wore to the guns and cannons that made mighty, hurtful roars, to their unusual language, everything was strange.

The Powhatans were curious about these people. They didn't know if they were gods sent down from their god, Okee, or if they were evil demons, like the white Spaniards in the south whom they had heard had ruthlessly tortured and killed their kin. They could not imagine that these foreigners, in the name of their rulers, the first Queen Anne and the first King James, would one day change their entire way of life, by peaceful means—or by force, if it proved necessary. But, for the lively, spirited Pocahontas, the visitors from "the edge of the world" were a source of endless fascination.

Different cultures will, inevitably, clash—especially when each knows little about the other. The Europeans believed the Native Americans were savages; they laughed because they liked cheap trinkets and were afraid of guns. The Indians, on the other hand, laughed at the foreigners for knowing neither how to plant corn nor how to use a tomahawk. They could not understand why these white men wore such uncomfortable attire, why they slept in dangerous beds from which they could fall onto the floor, or why they chose to live in wooden lodges.

Pocahontas became a bridge between the two worlds. It was

she who managed to keep war at bay. She not only saved John Smith's life, but she managed to get supplies to Jamestown during the lean months of winter, thus saving the settlement of foreigners from starvation and certain death.

Her story is one of adventure, a tale involving romance, friendship, and courage. But Pocahontas did not set out to become a "hero." She merely lived her life, interested in everything, bursting with spirit. But, in her endless curiosity and loving concern for others, she became a hero after all.

No one will ever know whether or not Pocahontas really lived through all the exciting adventures described in this book. But her life, her exuberant charm, and her special courage is not only the stuff of greatness, but the material from which myths are created—and endure.

KARLA DOUGHERTY

1995

VIRGINIA IN 1606—FROM CAPTAIN JOHN SMITH'S MAP

The Legend of
Pocahontas

CHAPTER 1

THE RETURN OF THE WARRIORS

THEY HAD NOT expected so much snow so close to spring, but the northeast woodlands of Virginia were covered with a thick blanket of white. The large white flakes were still falling as Opechancanough and his Algonquin braves trod silently through the forest. Hanging from their belts were the scalps of their enemy, the Monacan Indians, tokens of a recent battle.

But now, even in victory, Opechancanough was uneasy. During the vicious storm, snow had blown in their eyes, blurring their vision; it was possible that some Monacans had escaped unseen. Although they were very close to home, to the lodges of Werowocomoco, an ambush party could be lying in wait. They still needed to be on their guard, to look behind each tree for crouching figures, to listen to sounds so carefully that a squirrel could not crack a nut without their hearing it and pinpointing the bough where it perched.

Opechancanough led the long line of men that threaded its

1

way through the broad cutting between huge oaks, still covered with last year's bronze leaves. He held his head high and, silently, he composed the song of triumph he would sing to Powhatan, the powerful chief of the Powhatans and all the other Algonquin tribes. Then, suddenly, an arrow flew past, almost grazing his face.

At a shout from their leader, the long line swung to the right. Fifty arrows flew in the direction from which danger would likely come. But still there was silence, no outcry from an ambushed enemy, no sign of other humans.

Opechancanough consulted with his braves, trying to determine from where the arrow had come. As they talked, another arrow whizzed past his face.

"A bad archer," he muttered, "who cannot hit me with two shots." Then he pointed to a huge oak and commanded, "Bring him to me."

Two braves rushed to the tree. It was difficult to distinguish anything through the heavily falling snow and the mounds piled on the branches of tree. But then a moving shape could be discerned, and the two braves yelled in delight and disdain.

The white figure moved rapidly now. Swinging out on a branch and grabbing a higher one, he seemed determined to retreat from his pursuers to the very summit of the tree. But the braves did not waste time climbing after him; like panthers they leaped up in the air, caught the branch, and vigorously swung it back and forth so the feet of the archer slipped and he fell into their outstretched arms.

The warriors picked up the bundle of white fur, carried it to Opechancanough, and laid it on the ground before him. He knelt and lifted up the cap of rabbit skin, its flapping ears hiding the archer's face. Then he cried out in angry astonishment, "Pocahontas! What do you mean by this trick?"

The young woman, bundled in white fur, rose to her feet and laughed and laughed until even the oldest and most serious warrior could not help smiling. But Opechancanough did not smile. His dignity had suffered at the hands of this child, his niece, and the favored daughter of Powhatan. He shook her angrily. "What is the meaning of this, I ask you? What is the meaning of this!"

Pocahontas stopped laughing and answered, "I wanted to see for myself how brave you are, Uncle. I wanted to know just how great warriors such as yourself act when an enemy attacks. I am a good archer, Uncle. I would not shoot you. I aimed past you. But it was such fun to sit up in the tree and watch all of you stop so suddenly!"

Her explanation set most of the party laughing again.

"In truth, she is well named," said one of the braves. "Pocahontas, the little mischievous one."

"That is just my nickname. I have another name," she said to an old brave who stood nearest her. "Do you know what it is? Matoaka, Little Snow Feather, because always when the moons of *popanow*, of winter, bring us snow it calls me out to play. 'Come, Snow Feather,' the snow cries, 'come out and run with me and toss me up into the air.'"

Her uncle had now recovered his calm. He turned to the braves who had captured Pocahontas and commanded, "Since we have taken a prisoner, we will bear her to Powhatan for judgment and safekeeping. Had we shot back into the tree she might have been killed. See that she does not escape." Then he stalked ahead through the forest, paying no further attention to Pocahontas.

Not at all relishing their duty, the young braves looked sheepishly at each other and at their captive. Opechancanough was not to be disobeyed, but it would not be easy to hold the girl against her will. No force could ever be used against a daughter of the mighty Chief Powhatan.

Seeing their uncertainty, Pocahontas ran off. The two braves gave chase and caught up with her before she had gone too far. They led her gently back to her place in the line. But Pocahontas had not gotten her nickname for nothing. At first she walked along sedately, pretending to be unconscious of the braves' presence, waiting until they were off their guard. As soon as they seemed to believe she had resigned herself to the situation, Pocahontas sprang off and began running. Once again, she was captured and led back. She knew that the braves did not dare to bind her and she took full advantage of this, running first in one direction then in the other. And each time she ran away, the braves' comrades jeered and laughed.

The men no longer walked in line. They had advanced to a point where there was no longer any possibility of danger. Werowocomoco, their main camp, lay only a short distance away; already the smoke from its lodges could be seen across the cleared fields that surrounded it. The older warriors were walking in groups, talking about the brave deeds they had performed that day, and praising several of the young braves who had fought for the first time. Pocahontas and her two captors had fallen farther behind.

Though well satisfied with the results of her mischief, Pocahontas did not want to be brought into her home as a captive, even if it was half in jest. Her father might not consider it amusing and, even more, she did not like to be outwitted. She was so occupied with her thoughts that she forgot to continue her game and walked quietly ahead, keeping up with the longer strides of the warriors. Her two captors, their own thoughts occupied with their first war campaign, paid little attention to her.

Suddenly, Pocahontas stopped and bent over, pretending to fasten her moccasin. The braves kept walking, and by the time they realized that Pocahontas was gone, she had already hidden herself in a little hollow.

In the near dark Pocahontas's white fur was indistinguishable from the snow. The young men went after her, but before they reached the hollow, Pocahontas slipped back into the forest. As the daughter of the chief she knew every hill and glade of the land around Werowocomoco. Her captors, familiar only with her uncle's village, were no match for her. By the time they reached the snow-covered forest, Pocahontas had vanished in the darkness.

Opechancanough knew nothing of this escape. He was thinking about how he would caution his brother about how much mischief a princess could cause if she was not kept at home, occupied with tasks suitable to a girl of her age. She was lucky not to be the daughter of an ordinary brave, for then she would be forced to cook and clean and gather herbs all day. And even if Pocahontas was Powhatan's favorite daughter Opechancanough believed she should wait outside her father's lodge while he recounted the glorious deeds of his warriors.

As those warriors, members of the Pamunkey tribe, arrived at Werowocomoco, they beat their war drums and shouted. The noise roused the Powhatans, who came running to greet their allies and to rejoice with them in the victory against their common enemy, the Monachans. As runners sped ahead to Chief Powhatan's lodgings to advise him of their coming, the people of the village crowded around Opechancanough and his braves, asking many questions and admiring the scalps hanging from their belts.

The great Powhatan received Opechancanough not in his ceremonial lodge, but in the one where he usually slept and ate when at Werowocomoco. Before entering the lodge Opechancanough paused, turned to his men, and said, "Bring Pocahontas when I tell you to. We shall see what Powhatan thinks of a princess who plays dangerous games with warriors."

As Opechancanough entered the lodge, he could see his brother standing before the center fire. Powhatan was seated; at either side of him sat one of his wives. As his eyes adjusted to the dim light, Opechancanough saw that his nephew Nautauquas and Cleopatra (as the English later pronounced the girl's strange Indian name), Pocahontas's younger sister, were there as well. They had just finished supper and behind them in the shadows the dogs were gnawing turkey bones that had been thrown to them. Crouched at Powhatan's feet Opechancanough saw a child, clad a dark robe, the face hidden.

Powhatan solemnly greeted his brother and gestured for him to be seated. Soon the lodge was filled with braves. Those who could not fit crowded around the opening, relaying the conversation to the men and women who stood outside.

Proudly, Opechancanough began to relate the story of his bloody battle with the Monachans. Powhatan nodded in approval, now and then uttering a word of praise. When Opechancanough had finished his recital, the *shaman*, or medicine man, rose and sang a song in praise of the brave Pamunkeys, brothers of the Powhatans.

Then, one after another, Opechancanough's braves related their personal exploits.

"I," sang one, "I, the Forest Wolf, have destroyed my enemy. Even as the sun set in the red skies between the trees, I still gave chase, catching three Monachans by the banks of an icy blue stream that soon flowed red."

As each warrior told of his deeds, he was rewarded with much clapping and many murmurs of approval.

Powhatan ordered his people to open the guest lodge and to prepare a feast for the victors. Then Opechancanough rose again to speak. As he finished one more song of triumph, he turned to Powhatan. "Brother," he asked, "how is it that your warriors remain in their lodges leaving young girls who cannot distinguish friend from foe to guard your lands?"

Powhatan stared at his brother in astonishment.

"What do you mean by such a strange question?" he asked.

"As we returned through the forest," explained Opechancanough, "before we reached your boundaries and had reason to believe that some of the Monachans might still lie in ambush for us, an unseen archer shot at me, narrowly missing my face. It happened again before we captured the archer in the branches of an oak tree, and who do you think it was we found? A young Indian girl!"

"An Indian girl?" repeated Powhatan in surprise. "Is she from this village?"

"She is, indeed, Brother. She is waiting outside, to hear how you would judge a girl who thinks she is a boy and behaves so irresponsibly that she endangers the life of your brother." Opechancanough turned to his men. "Bring us the child," he commanded.

But no one came forward, neither the young braves nor Pocahontas.

Suddenly the little figure crouched at Powhatan's feet rose and stood in the firelight which shone on her face and long dark hair. "Did you want me, Uncle?" she asked.

"Pocahontas!" exclaimed Opechancanough in amazement. "How did you get here? And when did you have time to put on that dark robe?"

"Pocahontas can run even better than she can shoot, Uncle," she replied.

"What is the meaning of this, Matoaka?" asked Powhatan, making use of his daughter's given name. His voice was low but it was so stern that Cleopatra shivered, happy that she was not the one who had misbehaved.

"It was only a joke, Father," answered Pocahontas. "I meant no harm." She hung her head and waited for him to speak again.

"I do not permit such jokes in my land," he said angrily. "Remember that."

With a gesture and a whispered word of command he sent the Pamunkey braves off to the guest lodge. Opechancanough, still angry that a child could make such a fool of him, stayed behind. "Will you punish her?" he asked his brother.

"Of course I will," Powhatan answered. "Go to the guest lodge now and I will join you there soon. You go too, Nautauquas, my son. Carry my ceremonial pipe with you."

As she stood before him with her head lowered Powhatan looked thoughtfully at his daughter. Pocahontas waited for her father to speak, but he kept silent, so she turned and looked straight into his face. "Father," she asked, "do you know how hard it is to be a girl? My brother Nautauquas is a swift runner, but I am faster. I can shoot as straight as he can, though not as far. I can go without food and drink just as long as he can. And I can continue to dance long after he has begun to pant with tiredness. Yet Nautauquas will be a great brave and I . . . I must remember that it is my destiny only to be a good 'woman.' It is too hard, Father! Why did you give me strong arms and legs and a spirit that will not be still if I am to be only a wife? How can you blame me, Father, if I must laugh and run and play."

As she spoke, Pocahontas knelt and hugged her father's ankles. When she had finished she smiled fearlessly into his face.

Powhatan tried to remain stern in the face of his daughter's plea. As a chief he always listened fairly to the excuses offered by every offender who was brought before him. He judged each one justly, if sometimes harshly, but always with their explanations in mind. This child of his was as precious to him as a cool running stream is to a thirsty hunter on a hot summer day. If at times her spirit led her into mischief should he be angry?

Sensing that her father's anger had softened, Pocahontas stood up and laid her head against his arm. She knew that the mighty Powhatan loved her the most of all his children. When he raised his hand to stroke her cheek, Pocahontas knew she was forgiven.

"Your uncle is very angry," he said.

"But if you had seen him, Father, when the arrow flew by!" said Pocahontas, laughing at the memory.

"I have promised to punish you," her father said in reply.

"Yes. I know," she answered, unafraid.

"This is your punishment then," Powhatan said in mock solemnity. "With your own hands, the ones that so dislike sitting still, you will embroider me a robe of raccoon skin with quills and bits of precious shells."

Pocahontas laughed. "That is no punishment," she said, "because when I am asked to do things I do not like for those I love, then it is a pleasure for me to do them. I will make a robe for you more beautiful than any you have ever seen. Oh, how beautiful it will be! I will make patterns that no one has ever before dreamed of making!"

Pocahontas bit her lip and paused. "But, Father, you will never really be angry with me, will you?" she asked. "Let us make a pact. If I should at some time do something that displeases you, forgive me at once. And to show me that you are no longer angry put on the robe that I will make you. It will be a secret signal between us that you have forgiven me and that you will grant me whatever I wish."

And Powhatan promised. Then he smiled at his daughter and set out for the guest lodge.

CHAPTER 2

POCAHONTAS AND THE MEDICINE MAN

One unusually hot day, early in the spring of the following year, every Powhatan man, woman, and child was to be found out-of-doors, either working or playing. It seemed more like a day in late summer, when the corn is already standing tall and straight. But the corn-planting ceremony had only just been held, accompanied by the songs and dances of the tribe's sacred ceremonial rites. The tiny new leaves of the walnut and persimmon trees around Werowocomoco gently unfurled in the hot sun.

The children picked flowers, tied them together, and tossed them back and forth like balls. Others they twined into garlands for their hair. The older women of the tribe picked roots and leaves to use as dyes for *pemmenaw*, the grass cloth they spun.

The young boys of the tribe played at being hunters, pretending that their dogs were "bears" and "wolves." But instead of playing their assigned roles, the pets frolicked and leaped in delight around their young masters. The older warriors sat in front

10

of their lodges, some of them resting in the sun while others were occupied in making arrows, fitting handles to stone knives, or knotting crab nets.

Two prisoners, taken in battle against an enemy tribe, had been set to work making a Powhatan log boat. They were hollowing out a freshly cut oak log that, judging from its size, probably had been only an acorn when Chief Powhatan himself was just a papoose, some seventy years before. First the prisoners burned off a portion of the outer bark and then began hacking at the heart of the log with sharp flint axes.

The wives of the braves were also enjoying the outdoors, chatting as they worked. Some were scraping deerskins to soften the hides before they were cut into robes or moccasins. Here and there, little puffs of smoke were rising from small piles of heated stones under which the women were cooking the main meal of the day.

Pocahontas sat on a small hill overlooking the village. The chief's daughter joined the wives and maidens chatting in front of their lodges only on special occasions, as an honored guest. But Pocahontas was not alone. Whenever she wanted company, as she did on this beautiful day, Pocahontas surrounded herself with some of the young girls from the tribe. They obeyed her command not so much because she was the daughter of their chief but rather because she was likable and full of fun. Cleopatra, her youngest sister, sat beside her, trying to coax a squirrel on the branch above them to eat some dried corn from her hands.

Pocahontas had spread a robe of smooth raccoon skin across her knees. She had already painted it with a wide border. Along the edge of the skin, she was embroidering a deep pattern of white beads made from seashells. Beside her lay a reed basket filled with other beads, large and small, in colors of white, red, yellow, and blue.

"What does your pattern mean, Pocahontas?" asked the girl nearest her. "I have never seen another like it."

"Yes," said Pocahontas. "It is different from all other patterns because my father is different from all other chiefs. This song will tell you its meaning:

> Powhatan is a mighty chief,
> As long as the river flows,
> As long as the sky is above,
> As long as the oak tree grows,
> So long shall his name be known.

Pocahontas pointed to the raccoon skin. "Look here. This line is for the river. This one, that goes straight up, is the oak tree, and this long, wavy line is the heavens. I am making this for my father because I am so proud of him."

"But, Pocahontas," asked another of her companions, "why don't you use more of these red beads? They are so bright, like fire, like the blood of an enemy. Why do you use so much white?"

Pocahontas held her bone needle still for a moment, and thought.

"I cannot answer you exactly, Deer-Eye, except to say that I love the white beads best, just as I love to wear a white robe or a hood of white rabbit fur in winter. I always pick the white flowers in the woods, and I love the white wild pigeon and the white seagull best of all the birds. And I even love the soft white clouds above us better than the red and yellow ones that appear when the sun goes to sleep in the west. White is my favorite color."

The girls nodded as they continued to work their needles in silence. As midday approached, the day grew hotter, and Pocahontas began to feel tired. Down in the village the men had ceased their activities and lay stretched out in the shade of the lodges; only the women preparing dinner were still busy.

"Let's go to the waterfall," cried Pocahontas, jumping suddenly to her feet. "Go to your mothers and get some food to take with us. I will put away my embroidery and wait for you to return."

The girls raced down the hill while Pocahontas and Cleopatra returned the robe and the basket of beads to their lodge. A few minutes later they rejoined their companions and set off, laughing and running for a nearby stream. After walking for a while, they came to a place where the water rushed down a gentle incline to collect in a deep pool that was perfect for swimming.

The young girls took off their skirts and stood, hesitating for a moment, on the edge of the pool. Startled by their excited voices, mockingbirds burst into song in the oaks above them. In the bare branches of a dead sycamore tree, several raccoons lay curled in the sunshine.

Pocahontas was the first to jump into the icy stream, and her friends quickly followed, laughing, pushing, and crying out as they entered the chilly water. Only Cleopatra remained standing on shore.

"Come," Deer-Eye called out to her. "What are you waiting for?"

"The water is too cold for me," exclaimed Cleopatra. But before she could dress again, Deer-Eye splashed toward her and half-pushed, half-pulled her into the stream.

There was much screaming and calling as the girls slipped from the rocks into the pool and then clambered back to the rocks. The stream no longer felt so cold, and the dinner waiting for them in Werowocomoco was forgotten in the pleasure of their first bath of the season.

But then Deer-Eye, trying to pull herself back onto the rock, caught hold of Cleopatra's foot, pulling her off balance. Cleopatra slipped on the mossy surface below the stream and fell backward into the pool. She hit her head against a sharp rock and sank, unconscious, under the water.

Pocahontas immediately dove in after her sister. She felt around on the bottom, caught hold of her sister's arm, and pulled her to the surface.

With the help of the frightened girls, Pocahontas lifted her sister onto the bank. Cleopatra was bleeding from a cut on her head. Pocahontas tried to stop the bleeding with a piece of damp moss, but when this did not work, she turned to the others. "Run as if the Iroquois were after you," she commanded, "and bring me some strong branches. Hurry!"

Dressing hurriedly, they ran to obey her. With their knives, they cut several branches, tying them together with thongs torn from their deerskin skirts. They padded this makeshift stretcher with leafy branches, and then gently laid the unconscious Cleopatra on it. Pocahontas took one end of the stretcher, while her two strongest friends held the other side.

Silently they made their way through the woods toward home. Pocahontas's own heartbeats sounded in her ears as loudly as war drums.

They were still some distance from the village when they caught sight of Pochins, a tall medicine man known for his powerful *manitou,* or guardian spirt, which enabled him to communicate with the spirit world.

"Pochins, Pochins," cried Pocahontas. "Come quickly and help us! I am afraid my sister is dying. She did not wish to go into the water, but we pulled her in anyway and now she has cut her head and I cannot stop the bleeding!"

The medicine man was silent. He bent down from his great height to look closely at Cleopatra's wound. Then he took the end of the stretcher from Pocahontas and said, "I will take her to my prayer lodge."

The young girls turned and looked through the trees, toward Pochins's bark-covered lodge. Few people had ever entered that lodge and the girls shuddered with fear at the sight of it. No one knew what mysterious terrors might be found inside. Nevertheless, they bravely followed Pochins as he carried Cleopatra inside and gently laid her on the ground. He took some herbs from an earthenware bowl, moistened them, and bound them over the wound. Crouching at her sister's side, Pocahontas saw that the blood had stopped flowing. But still Cleopatra showed no sign of life as she lay there. Her hands and feet were damp, and although Pocahontas rubbed them vigorously, she could not make them warm again.

The medicine man then took a gourd rattle from another bowl. He placed a terrible scarlet mask on his face. Waving the children out of the way, he began to dance around Cleopatra, chanting in a loud voice and shaking the rattle until it seemed that the noise must wake even a dead person.

"My medicine is mighty medicine," the *shaman* shouted to Pocahontas. "Wait a little and you shall see the miracles it can do."

And, indeed, in a few moments Pocahontas felt the pulse in her sister's arm; she saw her eyelids flutter and felt her feet grow warm. And, as the shaking of the rattle and the shouting grew even louder and more frightening, Cleopatra opened her eyes and looked about her in astonishment.

"Mighty indeed is the medicine of Pochins," cried the *shaman* proudly, as he put aside his mask and rattle. "It has brought this maiden back from the dead."

Pocahontas bent to soothe her sister, who was terrified by what she had just seen and heard. She patted her arms and spoke to her as if she were a *papoose* on her back.

"Fear not, little one, no evil shall come to you. Pocahontas watches over you. She will not close her eyes while danger prowls about. Fear not, little one."

And Cleopatra clung to her, feeling safe in the arms of her sister.

By this time, the news of the accident had spread through the village and Cleopatra's mother came running, with several women, to the medicine man's lodge. Finding that Cleopatra was able to get up, they carried her home with them. Now that the fear had passed, the other girls remembered their empty stomachs and hurried off to find the dinner they had left behind at the waterfall.

Pocahontas did not go with them. She continued to sit on the ground beside the medicine man, watching him paint the mask where the scarlet color had worn off.

"*Shaman*," she asked, "can you tell me where my sister's spirit went while she lay there dead?"

"On a distant journey," he answered. "Therefore, I had to call very loudly to make it hear me and return."

"Who taught you your magic?" Pocahontas asked.

"The Beaver, who is my *manitou*, my spiritual guide, young daughter of Powhatan," he answered.

"And who will teach me? How will I learn?" asked Pocahontas, her head resting in her arms.

"You do not need such knowledge, since you are neither a medicine man nor a brave," said the medicine man. "I, Pochins, will call to Okee, our Great Spirit, if you ever need anything—food or clothes, or even a husband to take you to his lodge."

"But I would want to do that myself, Pochins," Pocahontas protested. "You do not know how many things I long to do for myself. Let me put on your mask and shake your rattle, just to see how it feels."

"No! No! Do not touch them!" Pochins cried, stretching out his hand. "The Beaver would be very angry with us and as punishment he would put an evil spell on us."

Pochins did not like children. His self-importance was so great that he never even noticed them as he strode through the village. But the eager look in Pocahontas's eyes seemed to draw unwelcome words out of him. He told her of the many days and nights he had spent alone, fasting, in the prayer lodge until some message had come to him from Okee, a message about the harvest or the success of a hunting party.

Pocahontas asked him many questions. She stayed with Pochins long after everyone in the village had eaten supper. The sun dropped out of sight and night came. Finally, as the moon drifted up over the trees, Pocahontas got up reluctantly from her mat, unbent her stiff legs, and made ready to leave.

She had learned many things from the medicine man, but there was one lesson that stayed in her mind, one that she had always known and believed: Pocahontas, daughter of the mighty Chief Powhatan, would create her own life. Her fate would be one that she chose—not one foretold by Pochins, by the Beaver, or even by Okee, the Great Spirit himself.

CHAPTER 3

MIDNIGHT IN THE FOREST

While Pocahontas and her friends were swimming at the waterfall, her brother Nautauquas took his bow and a quiver full of arrows and went searching for a deer.

Earlier, his mother had said to him, "You know that good luck comes to the hunter who wears moccasins and leggings made from the skins of the animals he himself has hunted. Your moccasins are old and worn. Bring me the skin of a newly slain deer and I will make you new moccasins and leggings."

After a short hike through the woods, Nautauquas came upon a pond covered with fragrant waterlilies. He hid behind a sumac bush and waited for a deer to come and drink. Soon enough, a buck with full-grown antlers stopped to take a sip from the pond. Nautauquas shot one arrow—and hit his mark.

Natauquas was anxious to return to Werowocomoco with the deer. Night was falling and he had not eaten all day. He could easily have killed a squirrel and roasted it, but he knew it was part

18

of a brave's training to learn how to fast, to get him through the times when game might be scarce. Nautauquas's mouth watered at the thought of the juicy meat he and his family would soon enjoy.

The night was dark, but now that the moon had risen, long streams of light shone down on the forest path. Looking up through the branches at the moon, Nautauquas thought about the strange tales he had heard about the moonlight and about the spirits who inhabited it and guided good people on their way in the dark.

Suddenly, right in front of him, Nautauquas saw a creature dancing down in the moonlight, whirling and turning. A pair of startled rabbits scurried off into some sassafras bushes nearby. Then, as if sensing that there was no danger, the rabbits sat up calmly, and watched as the dancing figure approached. Nautauquas also heard a voice singing, although he could not understand the words. Mystified, he wondered if the dancer might be one of the moon spirits. He slipped behind an oak tree and watched the dancer advance. As the figure drew nearer, Nautauquas saw that it was a young girl, and very much a flesh and blood one, at that. She was dressed in a skirt of white buckskin, which flapped against her firm brown legs, and a necklace of white shells that clicked as she spun about. In the branches above, a squirrel, awakened from its slumber, began to chatter, and a screech-owl squawked at the moon.

Nautauquas saw that there was something familiar about the dancer, so he was not really surprised to discover, when she turned about, that she was his sister, Pocahontas.

"Matoaka," he cried, stepping from the shadows. "What are you doing here alone at night?"

Pocahontas was not startled by the sudden interruption. Instead, she seized her brother's hand and pressed it gently.

"It is such a beautiful night, Nautauquas," she replied, "that I could not waste it sleeping in the lodge. I often come here when the night sky is filled with stars."

"You are not afraid of wild animals or lurking enemies, my little sister?" he asked affectionately.

"Wild animals would not hurt me, brother. One night, I approached a mother bear whose cubs were with her, and she did not even growl," Pocahontas replied.

Nautauquas did not doubt her word. He knew that there were certain human beings whom animals would not hurt.

"And enemies," Pocahontas continued, "would not venture so near the village of the mighty Powhatan."

Nautauquas could not argue with her logic. Instead, he spoke of something else. "I heard you singing, Matoaka. What was the song?"

"It is my own song, which I first sang many moons ago," she answered, "and I always sing it when I dance here at night." Pochantas began to dance again, moving first her head and hands, then her feet, and finally her whole body. She began to sing in a sweet voice:

> I am the sister of the Morning Wind,
> And he and I awake the lazy Sun.
> We ruffle the feathers of sleeping birds,
> And blow our laughter in the rabbits' ears,
> And bend the saplings till they kiss my feet,
> And the long grass till it bows obedience.
>
> I am the sister of the wan Moonbeam
> Who calls to me when I have fallen asleep:
> Come, see how I have bathed the world in white—
> So faint his voice no other ear can hear.
> And I steal away from my father's lodge,

And in the world only I am awake,
And bears and wildcats and the sly raccoon
And deer out of whose eyes there peer the souls
Of maidens who have died before they knew love.
And in the world only the horned owl knows
Enough to sigh and think that though we have no wings
Our speed surpasses that of the tree-dwelling birds of prey.

When she had finished, Pocahontas bowed her head. "Did you like my song, my brother?"

"It is a wonderful song, Matoaka. Someday you must sing it for our father." Nautauquas paused for a moment, thinking. "But it seems to me that you are different from other girls. They do not rise from their sleeping mats and venture out into the forest alone."

"Perhaps they do not have an arrow inside of them as I do."

Nautauquas had seated himself in the crotch of a dogwood tree and he looked down at his sister with puzzled interest.

"An arrow?" he asked. "What do you mean?"

Speaking slowly, Pocahontas answered. "I believe that within me is the spirit of an arrow—a special arrow that will make me go great distances and do great deeds. I am shot forward by some unseen bow. I cannot be still. As with any arrow shot by a great brave, the spirit of this arrow in me cries out: 'Now I shall speed away; now I shall cut through the wind; now I shall journey where no arrow has journeyed before; now I shall achieve the greatness that is my destiny!' "

Nautauquas shifted in the tree. "These are strange thoughts, little sister, especially for a young maid," he said as he lovingly stroked Pocahontas's dark hair.

"But I am so happy, Nautauquas," she went on. "I love the warm lodge, the glowing fire in its center, the smoke curling up toward the stars I can see through the opening above me. I love to feel little Cleopatra's feet touching my head as we lie there together. But then I feel the arrow within me and I must rise silently and silently go out. And if the dogs hear me, I whisper to them and they lie down once again." Pocahontas took a deep breath. She looked about her in the forest and bit her lip. "I love Werowocomoco, yet I also long to go beyond the village, to where the sky touches the earth. I love the tales of the beasts the elders tell, but I also want to hear the braves when they speak of war and ambushes. Springtime and the sowing of the corn are very special, but I also look foward to the harvesting of the corn and the fall of the leaf that signals winter."

Pocahontas spoke with great passion, saying aloud what she had only thought to herself before. She paused for a moment, fingering the shells of her necklace. She heard the call of an owl. She turned around and, leaning on her brother's knees, she said, "Tell me, Nautauquas, tell me the truth, since you cannot speak anything else. What spirit is in me that makes me like rushing water, like a stream that hurries forward?" Pocahontas shook her brother's legs and cried, "What shall I become?"

Nautauquas smiled. He lifted his face to the soft night breeze. He looked at the uncounted stars in the sky, and glanced for a moment at the moon. Then he looked down at his sister and whispered, "You will become something great, Matoaka. This I know." He smoothed some loose hairs from her forehead. "I do not know whether you will be a warrior or a princess who will command many tribes or a great prophetess. But I am certain that this arrow of your spirit will take you far."

Pocahontas breathed deeply. "Thank you for your words, Nautauquas, my brother. And thank you for not mocking me."

"Why should anyone mock?" he asked. "It is not strange that

an arrow should quiver when a wind blows—or that you should be swayed by the arrow spirit within you, Matoaka. Some day—"

Suddenly there came a piercing scream from the depths of the forest. Natauquas jumped down from the tree. He pulled an arrow from his quiver and fitted it to his bow, ready to shoot. Could it be, he wondered, that an enemy war party had made its way to Powhatan's village past other allied villages on the way?

Pocahontas stood, listening intently, her head bent to one side.

The scream came again. "That is no human cry," said Nautauquas, loosening his bow. "It is a wildcat in agony. Let us go and find it."

Brother and sister ran swiftly in the direction of the sound. Again the cry came to guide them, but after that there was only silence as they ran through the moonlight and the shadows of the trees.

Nautauquas stopped suddenly, so suddenly that Pocahontas, running behind, came up hard against him.

"It is down there at the bottom of the hill," he said, pointing. "It must be caught in a trap. Let us go down very carefully."

In the darkness, they clambered down through the overhanging bushes and rocks. At the bottom of the hill, the moonlight shone on the striped body of a large wildcat caught in a trap.

"Look!" cried Pocahontas. "There is another one over there in the bushes. We must have frightened it off. He has been trying to kill the one in the trap because it cannot defend itself."

"That is so," agreed Nautauquas, preparing to shoot the lurking beast should it decide to spring at them. But instead the animal crept quickly up the hill. The imprisoned animal was bleeding from a large wound on its back. Its eyes shone like fire in the moonlight.

"Poor beast!" exclaimed Nautauquas in sympathy. "If only he

would let me touch him, I would free him. Otherwise he will starve to death unless his enemy comes back to kill him first."

"Brother," said Pocahontas, "I will free him. And if you will cut a strip of hide off your leggings I will bind up his wound."

"Silly child," Nautauquas replied, laughing. "A wild beast needs no balm or cloth for his wounds. If he were free to drag himself to safety he would lick his injury until it healed. But he would bite your hand off if you tried to touch him."

"No, Nautauquas, he will not harm me," said Pocahontas. "Watch and see how quiet he can be."

Pocahontas knelt down just beyond the reach of the wildcat and began to whisper to it. Nautauquas could not hear what she said, but, to his amazement, he saw that the beast no longer whipped its tail back and forth and its great muscles began to relax. Nevertheless, the young brave caught Pocahontas by the arm and tried to pull her away.

"There is no danger, my brother," she reassured him. "Fear not. Do you remember old Chief Noughmass, when the bees swarm over his neck and hands? They never sting him, although he cannot tell you why. Neither can I tell you why wild beasts will not harm me, but I know they will not."

So Nautauquas, knife in hand and breathing deeply, looked on while Pocahontas, speaking in a low voice, moved closer and closer to the wildcat. Taking her own knife from her belt, she began to cut through the thongs of the trap that held him. One paw was soon freed, but the beast did not move to harm his rescuer. Then, when the other thongs were loosened and the wildcat was free, it moved, slowly and painfully, off into the woods, ignoring the two humans.

Nautauquas breathed in relief. "It is a wonderful gift, Matoaka, but I pray that you do not test your strange power too far. Yet I am glad the poor beast got away. I do not like to see such suffering. I shoot to kill only when necessary, for food and for skins, and I do it swiftly."

Brother and sister climbed back up the hill and started toward Werowocomoco.

The night was already far along and Pocahontas was growing tired. Seeing this, Nautauquas took hold of her arm to guide her. As they approached the spot where they had met earlier, they saw a human figure crouched low to the ground. Even in the fading moonlight, Nautauquas could see that it was an old woman. Pocahontas recognized her as old Wansutis, a gatherer of herbs and roots.

"What are you doing here, Wansutis?" she asked.

"Hah! The little princess and the young brave Nautauquas," cried the old woman, scowling up at them. She looked down again, examining the earth as she spoke. "I seek roots and leaves by the light of the moon so that the magic drinks will be stronger when brewed by old Wansutis. I found many rare plants tonight. It has been a lucky night, perhaps because the young princess was also out in the forest."

Now, all the children of the tribe were afraid of old Wansutis. They told each other frightening tales of how she could turn those she disliked into dogs, bats, or turtles. Even Nautauquas could remember how he had run from her when he was a little boy. Her expression was so ugly and so evil that, even though she did not completely fear her, Pocahontas had no desire to stay and talk. She started on her way again.

"And what is Pocahontas doing in the woods at night?" asked Wansutis, standing now and staring at the young girl. "Does Powhatan know that she has left his lodge?"

It did not please Pocahontas to be questioned in so bold a manner by the old woman and she did not choose to answer.

"Ah," Wansutis shouted after her. "So you will not answer me. You are too proud of your place as the chief's daughter and of your youth. But one day you will be an old woman like me, without teeth, with weak legs, and life will be a burden." Wansutis spit on the ground. "Then you will not be so proud."

Pocahontas stopped and turned. "No, Wansutis, I will not grow old. I will not let the day come when life shall be a burden. You cannot read the future, Wansutis. I shall always be as fast as I am now."

"Do you think to ward off old age with the potions I make from the roots I carry here," shouted the old lady, "in this bundle too heavy for an ancient crone like me to bear on her back? Hah! You shall have none of them."

Pocahontas stopped at once. Stooping, she picked up the bundle of roots and swung it onto her strong young shoulders.

"Come, Wansutis," she sighed. "Do not anger me with your nasty words and I will carry your bundle to your wigwam. You are right. It is too heavy for your old bones."

The old woman grunted ungraciously as she rose to her feet. The three figures moved on slowly through the forest, as Wansutis could only hobble along.

Nautauquas was sorry to see that dawn was approaching. He feared that Pocahontas would not be able to return to her bed beside Cleopatra unseen, and that she would be scolded by their father. Still, they walked with Wansutis to her wigwam and Pocahontas set down her bundle. Nautauquas then took out his knife, cut a hind quarter from his deer, and laid it on the old woman's hearth.

"She has no son to hunt for her," Nautauquas explained, as he and Pocahontas left without a word of thanks from the old woman.

As they came nearer to the lodges at the center of the village, they heard shouting from every side. Small boys and young braves were rushing to and fro, glancing eagerly right and left.

"I wonder what has happened, Nautauquas," cried Pocahontas. "Let us hurry."

CHAPTER 4

THE ENEMY CAPTURE

Although it was still early morning when Nautauquas and Pocahontas reached the center of the village, they found everyone
already up and about. Braves, maidens, and tribal elders alike
were talking in groups, their voices raised in excitement as they
looked out toward the waters of the Chesapeake Bay.

"What is going on?" Nautauquas called out to Catanaugh, his
brother, as he and Pocahontas joined the crowd moving quickly
toward the river.

"A messenger has just brought word that our allies, the Chickahominies, surprised a war party of Iroquois and overtook them,"
Catanaugh shouted in excitement. "They are coming now with
the prisoners!"

Excited by the news, Nautauquas left the carcass of his deer
alongside his wigwam and hurried to the riverbank. Happily for
Pocahontas, standing with Cleopatra and the other women from
her lodge, no one had notice her nighttime absence.

It was now almost light. The crowd at the riverbank grew larger. Children climbed onto their parents' shoulders to see what was happening. Six large log boats were approaching from downriver. But even with the prisoners in sight, the tribal members could not forget that the sun was rising and must be greeted with their customary ceremony. As they did every morning, two elders took handfuls of dried *uppowoc* from their pouches, and, turning in opposite directions, each walked in a large half-circle, scattering the tobacco on the ground in the shape of a large brown ring. Braves and women hurried to seat themselves within this circle. With uplifted eyes and outstretched hands, they greeted the sun who had come back to them to warm their fields and to make their young corn grow strong.

By the time the morning ceremony had ended, the dugouts had almost reached the beach. There was now much shouting from the shore to the boats and back again. Pocahontas slipped into a thicket of bushes and climbed to a higher point on the bank where she could watch the landing by herself. She clapped her hands as the courageous Chickahominies leaped ashore, twenty of them from every boat. As the crowd jeered and shouted at the three prisoners in each dugout, Pocahontas looked on eagerly, curious to see what kind of monsters these enemies of her tribe might be.

The eighteen prisoners were not bound. They stepped from the dugouts as proudly as if they were going to a feast in their honor, instead of facing possible death. Pocahontas had heard many stories about this enemy, the Iroquois nation. She noted certain differences in the patterns, swirls, and colors of their tattoos and in the shape of their feathered and beaded headdresses.

The crowd followed the victors and their prisoners as they marched to the ceremonial lodge where Powhatan awaited them. Pocahontas slipped into the crowded lodge, even though one of

Powhatan's wives tried to stop her. She made her way without further opposition to the platform where her father sat, and she crouched on a mat at his feet where she could observe the goings-on.

One of the Chickahominy chiefs, whose face she remembered having seen at the great autumn festivals, was the first to speak.

"Powhatan, ruler of two hundred villages and lord of thirty tribes, who rules from the salt water to the western forests, we come to tell you how we have pursued your enemies, the Iroquois, the Massawomekes, who, two months ago, ambushed and killed a hunting party of our young men. We came upon them by the Great Swamp and, though they sought like bears to hide themselves in the swamp's murky places, I, Water Snake, tracked them down. Then I and my braves fell upon them, and now they are no more."

Murmurs of approval sounded throughout the lodge. Only the prisoners ignored Water Snake's recital, acting as if they were still hidden in the vastness of the Great Swamp.

"While we fought," continued Water Snake, waving his hands, "the white blossoms of the creeping plants turned crimson and the hungry buzzards circled overhead. We slew them all, Great Powhatan, all but the captives we have brought to you."

When Water Snake had finished, the shouts of approval from the crowd grew louder and did not stop until Chief Powhatan began to speak. In low and measured tones he said, "A tree has many branches, but only one trunk. Deep into the earth its roots stretch to suck up nourishment for every twig and leaf. I, Powhatan, chief of the Powhatans and its many tribes, am the trunk, and one of my branches is the Chickahominy tribe, which is very close to my heart. My children have done well. Chief Powhatan thanks them for their brave deeds. Now your young braves hunt unharmed and bring home meat for your feasts and hides for your clothes."

He paused and all eyes in the lodge were upon him. He continued, "You are asking yourselves, 'What shall we do with these captives?' And I answer: feast them first, so they cannot say that the Powhatan tribes are greedy and do not give to strangers. Then when they have eaten, let them die."

He waved his hand, signaling the end to his speech, and the news was shouted from the lodge to the eager crowd outside. Pocahontas knew from previous captures that the women were now hurrying about to prepare the feast. From where she sat on the mat, she could see some of the young boys trying to wiggle into the lodge on their stomachs. They wanted to see whether the captives showed any signs of fear.

Soon Chief Powhatan ordered the feast to begin. Everyone sat and waited for the food to be served so they could watch the prisoners eat. Then the women entered the lodge with large wooden trays and woven baskets laden with food. There were hot cakes of maize, wild turkeys, and fat raccoons. The captives were served first and none of them refused. They would not let their enemies see that fear of their approaching fate spoiled their appetites. So, after throwing the first piece of meat into the fire as an offering to the Great Spirit Okee, they ate eagerly.

Pocahontas noticed that one of the prisoners who sat nearest the front was only a little older than she was. He was too young to be a brave. She wondered if he had run away from home and had followed the war party, just as boys in her own tribe often did. She wondered if he was now regretting the eagerness for adventure that had made his first warpath his last.

When the prisoners had finished their meal, the women passed around bunches of turkey feathers so they could wipe the grease from their fingers. The captives were treated with the exaggerated courtesy that was customary towards those about to be put to death.

Powhatan then rose and, surrounded by several of his armed guards, he strode down the center of the lodge and out into the sunshine. Pocahontas followed right behind him and, once outside, ran to tell the curious Cleopatra all that she had seen.

"Why did you get to see it all," asked her sister jealously, "while all I could do was stand out here and listen to the shouting?"

Pocahontas laughed and pulled her sister's long braid. "Because my two feet took me in, dear sister. You are too fearful, little mouse."

There was a large open space before the ceremonial lodge. It was used for games and feats of running and shooting. Chief Powhatan, followed by his guards and his sons, approached the mound of firm red earth that rose several feet above the open area, and sat. The other chieftains and their wives took up their places behind them, either standing or sitting. The young boys sat in the branches of the only tree that stood within the limits of Werowocomoco. They looked with fearful longing at the slanting roof of the great lodge, which was undoubtedly the best place from which to see the upcoming events.

Pocahontas had no such fear. She simply ran to the opposite side of the lodge and climbed to the roof, where she sat comfortably, in the best place to see the spectacle that would soon take place.

As she sat and watched, Pocahontas saw two long lines of naked and boldly painted young braves, one composed of Powhatans, the other of Chickahominies, enter the open space below her. Facing each other they formed an aisle between them. Each man held bunches of fresh green reeds, sharp as knives, or heavy oak sticks, or stone tomahawks. For a moment, the braves all stood motionless, waiting.

Pocahontas recognized most of the men below her: Black Arrow, whose ear had been clawed off by a bear; Leaping Sturgeon, who had joined two war parties before the chieftains had even pronounced him old enough to be a brave; her own cousin, White Owl, the most wonderfully tattoed of them all; and Nansamond, the young chieftain who wore a live snake as an earring.

Finally, Powhatan gave the signal and the captives were led forward into the arena. They knew what awaited them. Each one of them, except perhaps the young boy, had himself given to others the same punishment that was about to befall him. Every brave knew that he might someday have to face the same fate. Singing courageous songs of triumph, the captives began their run down the awful aisle of death. And the blows rained upon them, on their necks, head, arms, and even their legs.

Pocahontas noticed with interest that the boy was last in line, and that he held himself as bravely as the others.

When they reached the end of the row there was no escape— no escape anywhere ever again. The prisoners were forced back down the same aisle of death, running so fast that it seemed as if each one escaped the blow meant for himself, only to receive the one meant for the comrade in front of him.

Pocahontas began to feel sick as she looked down upon them and saw their bloody wounds. At first she decided it was the hot sun that was making her ill, but when she noticed the boy she felt even sicker. He was almost at the end of his strength. A few more blows would finish him. Some of his elders had already fallen to the ground, unable to rise.

To her astonishment, Pocahontas found herself wishing the boy might not fall, that he might escape by some miracle. How can I think such a thing, she said to herself. Was this boy not an enemy

of her tribe? But she could not help closing her eyes when she saw
Black Arrow aiming a terrible blow at his head. She suddenly
remembered the injured wildcat she and Nautauquas had saved
the night before. But no one should ever pity an enemy. What
was she made of?

As Pocahontas opened her eyes again, she heard a woman cry
out. She saw old Wansutis rushing towards the injured boy.

"I claim this boy," Wansutis panted. "I claim him by our ancient right. Stop, braves, and let me have him."

The stunned braves dropped their arms to their sides, and the
panting, bleeding captives had a moment of reprieve.

Turning towards Chief Powhatan, the old woman cried again in
a loud voice, "I claim the boy to adopt as my son. Many winters
and springs have passed since my own sons were slain in battle. I
am old and feeble and need a young son to hunt for me. By our
ancient custom, I claim this captive as mine."

There was an outcry from the younger braves who felt robbed
of one of their victims, but the older chieftains on the hill de-
bated for a few moments before giving their decision: Wansutis
had the right to claim the boy. Chief Powhatan ordered two of his
guards to carry the youngster to Wansutis's lodge.

Pocahontas suddenly felt at ease again. Try as she might to feel
differently, she was *glad* the boy had not been beaten to death. As
soon as he was carried off, the beatings began anew. But Pocahontas had now had enough. It would continue, she knew, until
all of the captives were dead. She slid down from the roof of the
lodge and started toward Wansutis's wigwam. By the time the
others arrived, Pocahontas had already hidden herself behind a
rock where she could see right into the opening of the wigwam.

She watched the guards gently lay the unconscious boy down.
She saw Wansutis kneel and fan the embers of her fire until they

blazed up. Then she saw the old woman heat a pot of water, and then throw some herbs into it. This brew she used to bathe the boy's wounds, treating them afterward with acorn oil. While she worked, Wansutis prayed, pleading with Okee to heal her son, to make him strong again so that he could care for her in her old age.

Pocahontas crept closer to the wigwam so she could see whether the boy was still alive. When at last he opened his eyes, he looked beyond the hearth and the crouching Wansutis, straight into the gaze of Pocahontas. She put her finger to her lips; she did not want Wansutis to know that she had been watching. The touch of the old woman's wrinkled fingers had been as tender and loving as that of a mother, and Pocahontas felt sure that she would have been angered to know that her actions had been observed. Now that she had seen all that she had wanted, Pocahontas stole quietly away.

She wandered for a while through the woods, gathering honeysuckle to make a wreath, and then returned to the village. The arena was now empty; the captives were all dead and the spectators had gone home.

A few days later, when the young Iroquois boy had recovered from his ordeal, a ceremony was held to celebrate his adoption into the Powhatan tribe and the great Algonquin nation. He was now called Claw-of-the-Eagle. The other boys his age looked at him with envy. Had he not proved his valor on the warpath and under torture while they were still playing games? They followed him around, eager to do whatever he said, each one trying to outdo the others in sports when he was watching. The elders, too, had only good words to say about Claw-of-the-Eagle, and Wansutis was so proud that she now rarely spoke of evil medicine and spells.

Pocahontas wondered if Claw-of-the-Eagle liked his new life, and one day when she was running through the forest, she came upon him. He was kneeling to spy on a flock of turkeys he meant to shoot, but his bow lay idle at his feet and Pocahontas saw that his eyes seemed to be looking at something far off in the distance.

"What do you see, son of Wansutis?" she asked.

He looked up, but did not reply.

"Speak, Claw-of-the-Eagle," she said impatiently. "Chief Powhatan's daughter does not like to be kept waiting."

He recognized Pocahontas as the person who had been peering into the wigwam the moment he had regained consciousness after his ordeal. He spoke to her.

"I see the sinking sun, Princess of many tribes, the sun that journeys toward the mountains and the village I called home."

"But you are one of us now," Pocahontas said, kneeling down beside him.

"Yes, I am the son of old Wansutis," he replied, "and I am loyal to my new mother and to my new people. And yet Princess, every day I send a message via the sun to the village far away where they mourn Claw-of-the-Eagle. Perhaps someday it will reach them."

"Tell me of the mountains and of the ways of your people," said Pocahontas. "I long to learn about other folk and different customs."

"No, Princess, I will not speak of them," Claw-of-the-Eagle answered her, shaking his head. "You would not understand. You have never said farewell to your family forever. I wish to forget, not remember."

Although it was the first time that someone had refused to obey her, Pocahontas felt no anger. She was, instead, lost in thought as she rose, dusted off her skirt, and went on her way home. As she walked through the silent forest, she wondered what it would be like if she were never to see Werowocomoco, her father, or her own people, ever again.

CHAPTER 5

The Great Birds

After Claw-of-the-Eagle had been adopted into the Powhatan tribe, life in the village settled into its familiar pattern. Spring became summer and, as the humid breezes blowing off the Chesapeake Bay rustled softly through the forest, as the rushing streams slowed and warmed, Pocahontas found herself restless. She wanted to find a place where the air was cool and the waters in the stream icy and deep.

Then one day some warriors from her Uncle Opechancanough's tribe paid a visit to Chief Powhatan at Werowocomoco. They came in a boat loaded with the finest deep-sea oysters and crabs, and other delicacies harvested from the seashore. The gift bearers were making ready to leave when Pocahontas, breathless and eager, rushed into her father's lodge.

"Father!" she cried. "Please grant me a wish. The weather is so warm and I and my friends long for the cool air one finds only near the salty water. Please, please, I beg you, let us go to my uncle's village by the sea for a few days. Please, Father!"

Chief Powhatan did not answer at once. He did not like it when his favorite child left the village. Seeing that he was undecided, Pocahontas began to plead anew, telling her father how much she loved him and how much it would mean to her to go away for a few days. Powhatan could not resist his favorite child's persistence for long, and finally granted his permission. After thanking her father with a kiss and a hug, Pocahontas raced out of the lodge to get her finest string of beads and the long cape she would wear on the journey. She summoned her friends, and they soon joined her in the dugout along with her uncle's warriors, who rowed swiftly downriver to the ocean.

Pocahontas was received with much ceremony at her uncle's village. As a princess it was her due, and at such times as it was necessary, she had the wisdom and dignity to put aside her child-like manner and behave in a grown-up fashion. Her Uncle Openchancanough greeted her kindly.

Later, they sat down to a feast of bear steak and the delicious little fish Pocahontas so loved to eat. "Have you forgiven me?" Pocahontas asked her uncle.

"For what, my child?" her uncle asked as he bit into his steak.

"You remember, Uncle. For shooting at you with an arrow last winter."

"I remember nothing unpleasant about you, my little niece," he replied, drinking a cup of walnut milk.

"Well, I am sorry nonetheless," Pocahontas continued. "I am ashamed of my foolishness. I was only a child then.

"Do you see how much I have grown, Uncle," she continued, "like the corn after a rainstorm? Soon they will say I am ready for a husband!"

"And whom will you choose, Pocahontas?" her uncle asked.

"I do not know. I have no thoughts for any of that yet."

"Well, then, what are your thoughts right now?" Openchanca-nough asked, wiping his mouth on a clean turkey feather.

Pocahontas put down her fish and clapped her hands. "My thoughts are of all things, Uncle! Of everything—of flowers and beasts, of dancing and playing, of wars and ceremonies, of the new son of old Wansutis, of Nautauquas's new bow, of necklaces and earrings, of old stories and new songs, and of tomorrow's bathing and—"

Openchancanough held up his hand to stop his niece. "I do not think you have to worry that you have left your childhood behind you just yet." He smiled.

Later, when the fire had died down and the storyteller had grown drowsy, Pocahontas fell asleep, with her arm resting on an orphaned baby bear that her uncle had brought into the lodge.

Opechancanough stared at his sleeping niece, his thoughts elsewhere. He did not feel the same deep affection for children as his brother, Powhatan. He was as brave a fighter, but not as great a leader in times of peace. It bothered him when he had to defer to his brother or obey his commands. But he knew that only unity between the different Powhatan tribes would keep them strong enough in the face of their common enemy, the Iroquois.

But his envy and vanity were so great that, although he pretended otherwise, he still felt the sting of ridicule from Pocahontas's winter prank. In fact, had she come to visit sooner he surely would not have received her so kindly. But now there were much more important matters to occupy his thoughts. Strange stories abounded about strange men in even stranger clothes, men who came on winged birds from the rim of the world, men who talked friendship, but did not understand Indian ways. A child's prank was nothing compared to that and, besides, he knew that his brother cherished Pocahontas more than any of his wives or other children. He did well to receive her kindly and hospitably.

In the morning, after they had eaten, Opechancanough offered to send Pocahontas and her friends on a canoe ride to see the ocean waves at their highest, but Pocahontas declined.

"No, Uncle," she said. "Thank you for your offer, but my friends have never seen the sea. The sight of the splashing waves would scare them too much. All we ask is some food to take with us on a short walk. I know the way down to a shallow beach where we can splash in the calm waters and enjoy the cool breezes."

Opechancanough was secretly rather pleased that the girls preferred not to go out on the open water. He ordered that they be given the food they requested.

The village was within a mile of the beach, and with a large supply of dried meat slung on their backs in brightly colored baskets, the group soon started off. Some of the young braves watched the girls as they walked down the path to the water. They wondered what they would be like when they were older and the time would come for them to choose their wives.

Pocahontas led the way through wild rose bushes, sumac, and an occasional pine tree, whose lowest branches were still high above their heads. It was a day made for enjoyment and the girls had not a care in the world. They sang as they walked and joked with each other.

"Did the little bear, your bedfellow, scratch you?" one girl asked Pocahontas.

"Maybe," suggested another friend, "it was not a real bear cub at all, but an evil spirit!"

"Nonsense!" answered Pocahontas. "He was real enough. Here is a scratch from his claw on my foot," she said, pointing. "And I do not believe an evil spirit can have much power on such a beautiful day. Okee must have chased them all away."

As she spoke, the path suddenly turned and before them shone the silver mirror of the sea.

"Look!" cried Pocahontas. Red Wing, her nearest companion, fell flat upon the ground, burying her face in the sand in fright and amazement. The others stood in hushed awe, staring silently at the watery new world in front of them. Gradually, their curiosity overcame their fear.

"How far does the water go, Pocahontas?" asked one girl.

"Can canoes travel on it?" asked another.

"Do fish swim in it?" asked yet another.

"Can one find good oysters in its depths?" asked Deer-Eye, a girl whose appetite often made her the object of fun.

Pocahontas answered as best she could. But, even though she had seen the Great Water many times, it was still almost as much a mystery to her as it was to her friends. Today, however, she greeted the ocean like an old friend. She could scarcely wait to throw herself into the little waves at her feet.

"Come on," she cried, "let's hurry! It will feel wonderful and cool on our sweaty skin." As she ran towards the water, Pocahontas threw off her skirt, her moccasins, and her necklace, and then jumped into the sea.

The other girls had learned to swim in the river at a very early age, but they had never been in such wide-open water before, without close, protecting banks on either side. They were afraid to follow Pocahontas into this unknown. But soon they saw that she seemed quite safe and her delight overcame their caution, and they were soon at home in the gentle waves.

For nearly an hour they played, chasing and ducking each other, racing and swimming under the surface. When they grew hungry they thought about the food they had brought with them. But when they emerged from the water and were about to start a cooking fire, Pocahontas asked them to wait.

"Here," she said, "here is fresher food. Look what the tide has left for us."

To their great astonishment, they saw that while they had been bathing, the water had receded and had left little pools in the sand. Standing in one of them, Pocahontas stooped down and ran her hand through the mud, bringing up a soft-shelled crab.

"See," she cried, "there are hundreds of them for our meal! But be careful to hold them just so, so that they will not nip you."

Laughing and shrieking, the girls gathered a larger supply of crabs than they could eat. They found bits of wood and dried seaweed on the beach which they lighted by twirling a pointed stick in a wooden holder they had brought with them. They cooked the crabs, and after they had eaten their fill, they stretched out lazily on the sand and talked until they dozed off, one by one.

But Pocahontas could not sleep. Instead, she strolled a little farther down the beach, picking up fine, thin shells of transparent gold and silver, which she liked to make into necklaces. She found so many that she could not hold them all in her hands, so she sat down to string them temporarily on a long blade of grass. When she was finished, she lay back against a ridge of sand and watched the gulls as they flew above her, dipping down into the waves every now then to catch a fish. Far away a school of porpoises was circling above the waves, their black fins sinking out of sight, and reappearing as rhythmically as if they were dancing to some unseen drummer. Pocahontas wondered where they came from and where they and the gulls were bound. How wonderful it would be to move so rapidly and so easily through water or air! But she did not really envy them. Was she not as fast in her *own* element as they were in theirs? She pressed her hand against the warm sand, feeling the grainy softness of it. She stretched out her foot so that the little waves could wet it. Within her grew a feeling of love for all living things.

The afternoon was very quiet and peaceful. The sun was only a little past its midday point. The silence was broken only by the cries of the seagulls and the soft swish of the waves. Pocahontas thought that it would be very pleasant to fall asleep here with her friends, but if she did, she would miss the wonders of the world around her.

But although she thought she had remained awake, Pocahontas realized suddenly that she must have fallen asleep and was now dreaming the strangest of dreams. As she looked out at the sea, she beheld an extraordinary sight out against the horizon. Three great birds, doubtless created by some powerful medicine man, were skimming the waves, their white wings blown forward. They were so large that they almost touched the heavens. One, larger even than the others, moved swiftly ahead.

Never, in a dream or in life, had Pocahontas seen such birds. She jumped immediately to her feet and stood gaping in terrified wonder.

"I must be bewitched!" she cried aloud. "Some evil medicine has befallen me!"

She called out and the tone in her voice roused her sleeping friends as if it were a war drum.

"What do you see?" she asked them anxiously as they gathered around her, not believing that they too would see what she had.

"Oh! Pocahontas, we do not know!" they answered in terrified unison, huddling around her. "What are those strange creatures that speed over the waves? Where did they come from—the rim of the world?"

Pocahontas felt truly frightened for the first time in her life. She glanced once more toward the sea, and then turning, raced off in terror. Her friends, who had never seen her like this, only added to her fright with their own. None of the girls stopped running until they had reached the village.

When they caught sight of the frightened children, the women rushed out and tried to soothe them, but they could get no explanation of what had so startled them. Finally, Opechancanough approached the girls, and when Pocahontas tried to tell him what she had seen, his face grew stern and serious.

"It is as I feared," he said to one of his chieftains. "It seems the word which came from the uplands was true. It is a marvel that bodes only ill."

He began to give hurried orders. The dugout was brought up to the shore and Opechancanough waved Pocahontas and her friend into it with little ceremony.

"I will send a runner to Werowocomoco with news for my brother," he called out to Pocahontas as the boat swung out into the river. "He will reach the village by land more quickly than by river. Farewell, Matoaka."

And although she wanted to question her uncle about what it was he had heard and feared, Pocahontas was relieved to be on her way home to her people and to her village, where such strange sights as she just beheld never appeared.

CHAPTER 6

JOHN SMITH'S TEMPTATION

Had Pocahontas seen and heard what was being planned on the strange, frightening "birds" of the ocean, she would not have felt so safe sailing home with her friends to Werowocomoco.

For those strange "creatures" were not birds at all, but rather British sailing ships. For nearly five months the *Discovery*, the *Godspeed*, and the *Susan Constant* had been tossing about on the high seas, and finally had arrived at the broad mouth of the river where Pocahontas and her uncle first caught sight of them. The British sailors had already decided to name the river after their king, James.

As the white sails that had so terrified the Indians flapped idly in the breeze, the Englishmen sat in their captain's chambers, discussing where to erect the first permanent English settlement in America, in the place they now called Virginia, in honor of Queen Elizabeth, "The Virgin Queen," and which the Indians called Wingandacoa.

46

The ships had first set sail from England in December of 1606. Among the many men aboard were veteran explorers, seasoned sailors, and even novices who had never been away from home for longer than a day.

Among the veterans was one Bartholomew Gosnold. He had first sailed to the New World five years before, landing far to the north of the river where the three ships now rested. It was he who had discovered and named Cape Cod and Martha's Vineyard, off the coast of New England. Christopher Newport, captain of the *Discovery*, had also sailed before into Western waters, but farther south. He was a fierce enemy of the Spanish and he had sunk some twenty Spanish galleons during his travels. Many other men had made the journey across the Atlantic in the hopes of finding material gain or for the love of adventure. They had all heard the story of the lost colony on Roanoke Island, whose English inhabitants had mysteriously disappeared from the face of the earth. The British believed the disappearance to be the work of the Indians, but no one really knew. Neither could they know if a similar fate awaited them.

Also aboard the *Discovery* was John Smith, a soldier whose exploits in battle had already become legendary. Smith had also earned a reputation as an excellent bargainer who was expert at bartering trinkets and goods in exchange for cooperation from the Indians whose land the English had invaded.

The officers aboard the *Discovery* had to decide where to locate their settlement. They knew that it must be near enough to the coast, so that goods shipped from England would reach them with as little difficulty as possible. But they also had to be far enough inland to lessen the danger of attack by pirates and Spanish raiding parties. Further, the location had to be a healthy one, free of stagnant water. It had to be easily defensible should the

Indians prove unfriendly, as they were in other parts of the New World the British had tried to settle.

While Captain Newport and his men discussed their strategies, John Smith stood at the prow of the ship, paying scant attention to the conversation in the captain's cabin. Although he was not tall, he was powerfully built and even from behind, he looked like a man of action. His mouth was hidden by a long beard and mustache, and there were deep lines around his nose that belied his twenty-eight years. But his brow was high, wide, and unfurrowed, and his hair and eyebrows were thick and dark. He had, overall, the intelligent, eager countenance of a man who had seen much of the world.

Standing by the ship's rail, John Smith slowly moved his spyglass in every direction. He had swept the river and both shores as far as his eye could see and now he rested his sights on an island a little distance away, near the right-hand bank of the newly named river. From this distance, it appeared to be exactly the place they were looking for to build a settlement.

But Smith was soon distracted by a sailor who pushed through the crowd surrounding the cabin door. "Captain Smith," he said, "Captain Newport requests your presence in his cabin."

John Smith put down his spyglass and turned toward the Captain's cabin. He wondered what would be decided in the next hour. He wanted a chance to plant and nurture the seed of a new colony in this new land. He had faith in his own power to organize and to command men. Like other explorers before him— Raleigh, Drake, Sir Humphry Gilbert, and Sir Richard Grenville —he was bold, fearless, and untiring. The others had sought a northwest passage to India, a shortcut to the treasures of the New Indies. They had wanted to discover new lands and great riches before their Spanish enemies did. Yet among them, only Smith saw clearly the value of a settlement in Virginia, and the great

The white figure moved rapidly.
Page 2

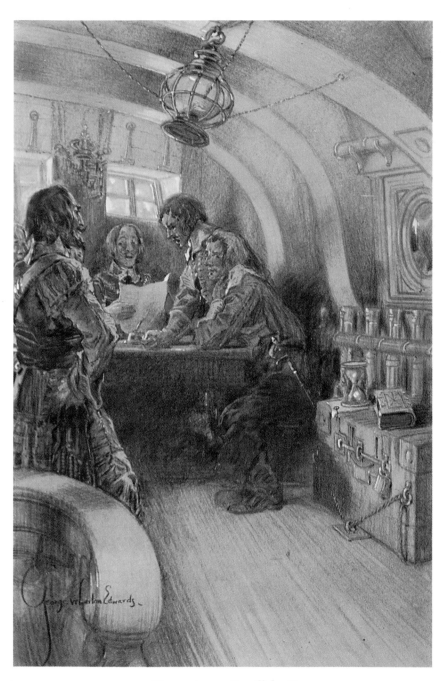

"Jamestown it will be!"
Page 49

opportunities that would arise from such a settlement. And he also saw quite clearly how the greed and petty jealousies of many of his fellow travelers could threaten its growth—and its very existence.

It was with a heavy heart that John Smith entered Captain Newport's cabin, although his face betrayed no emotion. Indeed, he was still consumed by the hope that he might be the one chosen to organize and lead the building of the Virginia colony.

Upon entering, Smith encountered little warmth—and only a few nods of greeting. He saw Captain Christopher Newport, Bartholomew Gosnold, Edward Wingfield, and several other veteran explorers seated around the cabin. From their expressions, he knew they must have been talking about him before he entered—and most likely not with approval. He took a seat in silence.

The men gathered in the room made up a powerful Council which had been designated by secret royal instructions when they sailed. This Council was now required to elect one man as president of the colony for the coming year. Smith knew that the Council members were jealous of him because he had achieved so much at such a young age. He was sure that he would not be elected to the post.

And he was right. The Council had made its decision while he had been absent from the cabin. Edward Wingfield would be the first president of the Virginia colony and Smith had not been chosen for even the smallest office. The others watched his face, hoping to see disappointment, but Smith showed none. Instead, he rose to his feet. "Captain Newport," he said, "and gentlemen of the Council. Permit me to suggest that we name this new colony after our gracious sovereign, King James."

To disagree would have meant treason. Therefore, in this the Council was compelled to follow John Smith's lead. Every man rose to his feet and shouted, "Jamestown it will be!"

The next point of discussion was the location of the settlement, and about this, everybody began to talk at once. Some wanted a site nearer the bay; others advocated exploring the other rivers nearby. But Newport, eager to be done with business and to return to England, shouted them all down.

"We choose today!" he cried, bringing his fist down on the table with a bang.

The majority was in favor of the island that Smith had been examining through his glass. It was large and level and not too far from the sea. Smith remained silent during this discussion. He knew that if he showed enthusiasm for this choice, the island site would be voted down—and Smith felt certain that the island was the perfect place for Jamestown. When asked what he thought of the island, Smith said only, "It has much to commend it."

"It is settled then," said Captain Newport, rising from his chair. "Let us go ashore without delay to mark out the site of our new Jamestown."

After some debate, the Council chose places for the government house, the church, and the community storehouse. Some of the men were soon busy felling trees and clearing spaces for temporary shelters. The matter of a fort was yet to be discussed, but Smith knew it was important. His vast military experience told him that without a fort, the island was vulnerable to attack. But he remained silent, waiting for the time when such a suggestion would be acceptable to the Council.

Meanwhile, Smith strolled alone through the tangle of undergrowth and flowering vines where mockingbirds and catbirds darted. He stopped at the side of the island nearest the mainland.

"Here," he said, speaking aloud to himself, "here, on this side, should be the fort . . . and a high tower from which we could see our enemies. And there, to the right, a strong protective wall to preserve our homes—"

Smith stopped suddenly. His vision of a mighty fort, a strong and healthy settlement, would not change things. He admitted to himself that he was disappointed—he had wanted to be president of the new settlement. He *deserved* to be president. He had just resolved to sail back to England on the *Discovery* when three loyal friends—Dickon, Hugh, and Hob—approached him.

"Captain," Dickon whispered, "we would like a word with you."

Smith looked curiously at his friends. "Of course," he replied.

"It was a dirty trick that you weren't named president," Hugh cried. "We all know you deserved it!"

"That is right," added Hob, "and we are ready to fight for you. We can gather enough support to make Wingfield step down so you can take your rightful place!"

It was a tempting offer and Smith was deeply touched by the loyalty of these three men—expressed at a time when he needed it most. It was not power that he wanted, nor was it an issue of vanity for him. He simply knew that he could help the colony grow and develop far better than anyone else. This he believed with all his heart.

But just as he had decided to accept this mutinous plan, an arrow flew by his ear and fell at his feet.

"Indians!" cried Dickon.

Smith looked toward the woods beyond the water and thought he could see a figure half-hidden behind a birch tree.

"We had better go back and warn the Council," he said, turning. "I do not think they will attack if we stay together."

Smith stood a moment lost in thought. "That is it, my friends," he said. "That is it: *if we stay together!* We must forget our recent discussion. We must stand together, men, here in this new world. We must be united to avoid Indian attacks—and that means we must respect the wishes of the Council and President Wingfield."

Although his friends would have preferred to fight, the men realized that Smith spoke sense, and agreed to abide by the Council's decision for the good of the colony.

When they returned to the building site, Smith told President Wingfield about the hidden bowman and warned him of the danger to anyone who might straggle away from the group. But the members of the Council refused to believe that the Indians were not friendly and that they needed a fort for protection— especially because this advice came from John Smith.

Instead, the men spent their days clearing the ground and setting up tents. They were all so tired of the cramped life aboard ship that they were glad to stretch themselves out on the earth and sleep under the stars.

Smith decided to set an example for some of the English gentlemen who stood about with arms folded as they watched those below them in station work hard at building the colony. He swung his ax, wielded his hammer, and labored rhythmically with his saw. But he was still far from happy with the situation in Jamestown, and when an opportunity arose to leave the island, he took it.

With Captain Newport and twenty others, he set out in a small boat to explore the upper part of the James River. The men were gone for several days, traveling as far as the great falls outside a Powhatan village.

On their return to Jamestown, they were greeted with the grave news that during their absence the Indians had attacked, killing a boy and wounding seventeen others. Luckily, a shot fired from one of the ships had so terrified them that they had run for the woods before doing further harm.

The Council was now forced to recognize the need for some

protection, and they ordered everyone to stop their work and concentrate on the building of a strong fort—just as Smith had suggested upon their arrival.

Suddenly, danger seemed to lurk behind every tree, down every path, along every section of the riverbank, and the men worked quickly to build their fort.

CHAPTER 7

A FIGHT IN THE SWAMP

Fear takes no sides. Just as the colonists feared the Indians, the Indians feared them. The Englishmen spent the spring months putting their settlement in order. At Werowocomoco, not a day went by without new rumors about the white strangers and their curious habits. What did the palefaces eat? What were the games their children played? What were their strange weapons that made so much noise? Why did they wear so many layers of clothing?

Most of the rumors filled the Powhatans with dread. Were these white strangers gods who lived charmed lives, immortal beings who could not be felled by an arrow or a medicine man's spells?

This fascination was fed by the old wise men of the village. Around the nightly campfires the elders related ancient prophecies of palefaced heroes who would teach the Indians how to harvest and hunt better. They told other stories that sent shivers of fear through the Powhatans, stories about tribes far to the south who had lost their land and their loved ones at the hands of the Spanish palefaces who had brought fighting and fire to the peaceful land of the West Indies. These invaders were called "white demons," because they left terrible disease and death wherever they set foot.

Chief Powhatan and his Council knew that they must learn the truth about the newcomers before the rumors caused widespread panic among their people. They had to know if these white strangers were evil gods or mere mortals and then deal with them accordingly. The only way to find out would be to shoot an arrow into a white man and see whether or not he fell. If an arrow wounded, then he could not be a god.

The Powhatans painted themselves in the age-old way to ward off evil and give them strength and confidence. They took their bows and arrows and bravely set forth, ready to test the "gods" in Jamestown. And with the arrows that slew the young boy and wounded seventeen settlers, the Indians proved to themselves that the white strangers were indeed mortal. So the frightened colonists built their fort against further attack. At the same time, the Powhatan tribe lost its fear of the white men and began to plan its fight against them. They now knew they needed no medicine to ward off evil spirits; they needed no paint or rattles to scare off unwanted gods. These colonists, they now understood, were only human beings. They could be shot and killed—and were not safe in the shadow of Okee or any other Great Spirit. Against gods, the Indians could not prevail. But these strangers were mortal, men who felt hunger and thirst and pain. Now the question became what to do? How would they drive the white men from the land?

As they sat around the fire, smoking their pipes and thinking, many of the Powhatan elders urged immediate steps.

"It is easy," said one, "to pull up a young oak sapling, but too hard to uproot a full-grown tree."

Chief Powhatan's son Nautauquas was among those most eager for action. He had already come to be known as a great brave and a mighty hunter despite his youth. Now he saw a new way to distinguish himself: to go forth into battle where there were dangers he could not even imagine. He did know now what magic these palefaced strangers used to protect themselves. But if he and his band should overcome them and wipe away all traces of their short stay, he would become a hero. His exploits would become a tale for winter firesides and a song for singers of brave deeds.

"Let me go, Father," he pleaded. "You who have conquered thirty tribes, let this fame be won by your son."

"Wait!" was Powhatan's only answer.

The medicine men and the priests had advised Chief Powhatan to wait and watch. Even though they had fasted and prayed to Okee to reveal to them what they must do, no one yet knew the intentions of these palefaces.

In spite of his years, Chief Powhatan also felt the urge for action, and his heart leaped when his son gave voice to his own wishes. He longed to take to the warpath, to slip through the forest, to spy upon the strangers who had dared make a place for themselves in his land, and then to fall upon them, terrifying them with his awful warcry as he had terrified so many of his enemies.

But he dared not do this yet. Powhatan was not only a great war chief, but also a peaceful leader of his people. Okee had not so far given any sign—and the white men with their strange faces and stranger tongues might yet, of their own accord, acknowledge his sovereignty. There might not be a need for war or the sacrifice of his young braves.

"Wait!" Powhatan said again to his son. "We must wait and see what these strangers mean to do."

When Nautauquas came out of his father's lodge, he took his bow and arrows and went off to hunt. He could not bear, in his disappointment, to hear any more words. He longed for action. He ran swiftly through the forest and soon reached a spot where he was sure he would find a flock of wild turkeys. But, suddenly, there in front of him was his sister, Pocahontas. She too was hurrying, intent on some errand that fully occupied her because she did not stop to watch the birds or to pull up any flowers as she usually would do.

"Matoaka," Natauquas called. "Where are you going?"

"To see the strangers and their great white birds again, brother," she replied. "I cannot rest until I am able see what they are like close up. They are all I think about, day and night."

"But remember what our father said," her brother cautioned her. "No one is allowed to go near the strangers' island!"

"Oh, my father does not mean those words for me," she proudly answered. "You know he lets me do things that are forbidden to others."

"But not this, little sister," Natauquas warned. "He just now forbid me to go there. His mind is set. Do not tempt his anger. Even though he loves you well, he will punish you if you disobey him. Turn back with me, Matoaka. Please. Come now and help me to shoot some wild turkeys."

Pocahontas was reluctant to give up her long-planned expedition, but she finally agreed. She remembered when Chief Powhatan had ordered one of his wives to be beaten because she had disobeyed him. It was better not to test him too greatly. Besides, it would be fun to hunt with Nautauquas and see which of them brought down more turkeys. The tribe needed food, and the women had been complaining that the braves had become far too lazy of late.

While Pocahontas and Nautauquas were busy snaring turkeys for the tribe's larder, the English settlers in Jamestown were scrambling to find enough food to feed themselves. Their food supply, musty and moldy from the long journey overseas, was growing scarcer every day. They did catch some of the fish which were plentiful in the river, but they were growing weary of fish, day after day. They hungered for some juicy English roast beef.

Patience and self-control had prevailed between the Indians and the settlers and there was now an unspoken truce of sorts. Chief Powhatan's tribes were willing to trade corn and venison for the strange and wonderful objects the English had brought with them—mirrors and compasses and the softest silks. But the Powhatans visited Jamestown less and less. The English never knew when the Indians would appear, and lately there had been no visits at all.

John Smith, known for his ability to bargain and wheedle—or to use force, if necessary—left Jamestown more than once to go up the various rivers in search of supplies.

But the situation was now very serious indeed. Food was more scarce than ever and even the fish were not biting. The settlers were literally starving to death. Something must be done at once, and during an emergency meeting of the Council, John Smith spoke up.

"Gentlemen of the Council," he began, "there is only one thing to do. Since our larder will not fill itself, we need to take matters into our own hands. We have had this problem long enough. Give me a few good men and one boat, and I will set off north, up the river the Indians call the Chickahominy and, with good luck, I will come back with provisions enough for all of us—

and with a permanent treaty with the Indians to keep us supplied until our own crops have grown."

The Council readily agreed—they had no choice. The boat was soon filled with a supply of beads, cloth, and other bright, colorful articles from England. Soon enough, Smith set off with the good wishes of the hungry colonists.

After they had reached what seemed to Smith a good spot for trading, he took two men, Robinson and Emery, and set off to further explore the narrowing river. He ordered the others to wait for him and on no account to venture nearer shore where danger might lurk.

It was quiet as they rowed the canoe through the peaceful waters. John Smith was glad to be away from the noise of his complaining men, from the cries of the hungry people at Jamestown for whom he could do nothing. He felt no fear as he listened to the soothing rustle of the leaves and the rhythmic dipping of the canoe paddles. Smith in the company of his two friends had absolutely no fear of what the forest might hold.

The three kept to the middle of the stream to be safe from any arrows that might be shot at them from shore. But hours passed and nothing happened, and Smith, now hungry and tired, grew weary of the monotony. He decided to explore a bit on land. To his experienced eye, an inlet which they had just passed seemed so suitable a place to land a canoe that he felt sure an Indian village must not be too far away.

"Drop me off there, at that inlet, then push out into the stream again. Wait for me." With those words, John Smith jumped out of the canoe and strode into the forest, ready for either friendship or battle with the Indians—whichever he might encounter.

After a brief walk he came to a clearing. Suddenly, as if they had been following him, two hundred painted Indians came out of the woods, shrieking and shooting their arrows wildly in all directions.

"War then!" cried Smith aloud, and as one young brave in advance of the others stopped to take aim, Smith leaped forward and caught him. Ripping off his own belt, Smith bound the astonished Indian to his left arm so that he could use him as a shield. Thus protected, he fired his pistol, and the ball entered the breast of an older chieftain, killing him instantly. For a moment the strange fate which had overtaken the leader checked the onslaught. His companions stooped down, one behind the other, to examine the wound made by the demon weapon. This respite gave Smith time to whip out his sword, and whirling it about him, he kept his enemies at a distance.

He might have succeeded in defending himself this way for some time longer, for the Indians had stopped shooting, not certain whether their arrows would be effective against one with such a frightening weapon. But all of a sudden, Smith became aware of a new danger. The marshy ground on which he stood had softened under his weight and that of his living shield and he now felt himself sinking deeper and deeper into the morass until he was submerged up to his waist. The Indians, still fearing that he had some other strange weapons or evil medicine in his power, did not rush forward to attack him.

The day was bitterly cold, and the stagnant water chilled him to his very bones. Smith's teeth began to chatter, not with fright, but with cold. It was almost with a sense of relief that he saw the Indians start toward him. Carefully treading in their light moccasined feet, they gradually surrounded him. Two of them took hold of him, while others loosened the bound brave. They then drew him up from the sucking earth by the arms.

Smith knew there was nothing to be gained by struggling, and he faced the Indians with no sign of fear. His captors led him to a fire which was blazing nearby, on firmer ground where a chieftain sat. This chief was Opechancanough, Chief Powhatan's brother.

At a command, the guards moved aside and the tall, broad Opechancanaugh walked slowly around Smith, examining him from head to foot.

The chieftain paused. Smith knew that now was the time to engage the man's attention—before he might give an order to kill him. Slowly, he pulled his heavy silver watch from his pocket and held it up to his ear.

Never had Opechancanough and his men felt such an awe of the unknown. For all they knew, the small sparkling circle in the white man's hand might contain a medicine more deadly than that of his pistol. They stood like children in a thunderstorm, not knowing when or where a lightning bolt might strike.

But nothing terrible came to pass. Then Opechancanough, in his curiosity, put out his hand for the watch. Smiling, Smith held it toward him in his palm and then laid it against the chieftain's ear, saying in the Indian tongue, "Listen."

Opechancanough jumped with astonishment at the ticking sound and cried out. "A spirit! A spirit!" he shouted. "He has a spirit imprisoned inside!"

One by one, the captors crowded forward to look at the "turtle-of-the-metal-that-has-a-spirit." There was much excitement.

To increase this feeling of awe and delay the order for his death Smith felt in his pocket again and this time brought out his traveling compass. It was made of ivory, and the quivering needle was pronounced by Opechancanough to be another spirit.

But suddenly, without warning, two of the younger warriors, who had evidently determined once and for all to discover if this stranger was vulnerable or not, seized Smith and dragged him swiftly to a tree. They threw a cord of deer thong around him, drawing it tight. Then they notched their arrows and took aim directly at his heart. "In one second it will be over," thought Smith, "my life, my adventure, my ambitions, and my troubles."

At the last moment, Opechancanough called out to the braves, holding up the compass. Frowning with disappointment, the young men loosened their captive, and Smith realized that it was again the chief's curiosity that had saved his life. Using the meager number of Indian words he knew and by means of sign language, Smith attempted to explain how the compass worked.

"See here," he said, pointing. "I turn it like this and the spirit in the needle stays to the north and will not be kept from it."

When everyone had looked at the compass, Opechancanough again took it in his hand, holding it as gingerly as he would have held a papoose. This was something precious and he meant to keep it—but he still did not know if it was dangerous. It would be wise to take the man who did understand it with him.

"Come," Openchancanough said. "Since you are able to understand our words, come and eat in our lodge."

Smith had no choice but to follow. There was a feast waiting for him, and the half-starved Englishman ate heartily for the first time since he had set foot in the New World. At least he had gained the strength to bear bravely whatever fate might await him.

John Smith's fate turned out to be weeks of traveling from village to village while Openchancanough displayed his captive and his wondrous gifts. Smith himself saw many amazing sights, including a treasure-house ornamented with exquisitely painted dragons, bears, and leopards, and guarded by priests. He saw braves and children and women, young and old, who smiled and crowded around him, fingering his clothes and pulling on his beard. He watched the Indians at their work, tanning hides and dyeing skins, painting their faces and tattooing their arms with the animal symbols which, to the Indians, meant strong medicine and protection.

Finally, the group approached a very large village. Dogs barked and children shouted as they neared the first wigwams. Men and women, as swift and as lithe as deer, came running from every direction.

Smith had arrived at Werowocomoco and he was about to meet Pocahontas and her father for the very first time.

CHAPTER 8

POCAHONTAS DEFIES HER FATHER

"Pocahontas!" cried Claw-of-the-Eagle, as he pointed excitedly to the outskirts of the village. "Look! It is your uncle and his braves. They have the white prisoner with them."

Pocahontas dropped Claw-of-the-Eagle's pouch, which she had been examining to see if he had been lucky with his latest hunt. "Wait for me!" she shouted, as she followed old Wansutis's adopted son towards the gathering crowd. Never in all her life had she wanted anything as much as she now wanted to see this stranger.

"What does he look like?" she called out, panting, as she ran swiftly to the head of the procession. There, walking behind her uncle, unbound and appearing to be unafraid, was the white man. Her eyes devoured every detail of his appearance. She was almost disappointed to find out that he had only one head and two eyes like everyone in Werowocomoco. Surely, beings that

64

came across the water on tall white birds would look different than she!

But there were visible differences, more than enough to satisfy Pocahontas. One of the first things she noticed was the man's beard, so striking among the cleanshaven braves who rubbed their faces smooth with sharp, rough stones. He was also much younger than she had imagined and his clothes were very strange. He wore a cloth vest and confining leather boots, pants and a shirt, and even a wide-brimmed hat! But, above all, there was that strange cast to his face and hands, a whiteness Pocahontas had never seen before.

John Smith noticed the staring Pocahontas. He could see that she had a special claim to distinction when he saw that Opechancanough gave her a nod of recognition. She was a tall, strikingly pretty girl, about thirteen. However, it was not her face that caught his attention. It was her energy, her sparkling eyes and the mischievousness in her smile. He could tell that she was confident and intelligent—and used to getting what she wanted.

But soon his eyes wandered to the other staring faces, to the village of Werowocomoco itself. He sensed that he had reached the end of his journey, that here in this large, solidly built, and busy village he would meet his fate. Perhaps he would come face-to-face with the great Chief Powhatan the Indians talked about at night, when they sat around their bright fires. Perhaps he would be set free—or perhaps he would die. . . .

These were the same thoughts that were occupying Pocahontas. What would her father do to this man? Would his paleface magic help him? She had heard enough stories about the brutal white men in the south and in the upper lands, and the need to destroy the ones who dared take over their land. She knew also that this was the first time her father would have to deal with these strangers. She could not wait to see what would happen.

She ran ahead to the ceremonial lodge and entered without challenge from the guards. After her eyes adjusted to the dim, smoky light, she realized that the stranger had been expected. Opechancanough must have sent a messenger to tell of his arrival, because all the tribe's powerful elders were gathered in the lodge, as was the magnificent Queen of Appamatuck, ruler of an allied tribe. Pocahontas's father was seated on his raised platform. He wore the rich raccoon-skin robe that Pocahontas had painstakingly embroidered for him. Everyone had painted their faces and arms with elaborate designs drawn with the precious *pocone* red found in the earth. They wore their formal headdresses adorned with bright feathers and beads. Pocahontas was sorry that she had not had time to dress for this important occasion in her new white buckskin skirt and brilliant white-bead necklace. Her brown, fringed deerskin skirt and yellow beads would have to do.

She looked around for Claw-of-the-Eagle and was sorry he had not been able to enter the lodge. It was so crowded now that the guards would admit no one else. But soon the spectacle began and Pocahontas forgot all thoughts of her friend.

The entrance to the lodge darkened and a great shouting went up from the crowd as Opechancanough strode in, followed by his prisoner.

Chief Powhatan sat in silence, watching from his raised platform, until Smith stood directly before him. After a brief pause, he spoke, and everyone fell silent.

"We have waited many days and nights to see you, stranger from across the sea."

Smith looked at Powhatan, a finely built man whom he judged to be about sixty years of age. He sensed the chieftain's power and it reminded him of a dignity he had witnessed only once before, in the great ruler, Queen Elizabeth of England.

He answered in kind. "I, too, have heard much about you, great

Chief Powhatan." He spoke slowly and distinctly in the chief's own language.

They both nodded, each acknowledging the other's politeness. Then the Queen of Appamatuck approached Captain Smith and held out a clay bowl full of water with which he was to wash his hands. Pocahontas leaned over eagerly, curious to see if the water would wash off some of his strange color. But even after Smith had wiped his fingers on the turkey feathers the queen held out to him, he remained the same color. So, Pocahontas thought to herself, he is not painted white.

At the chief's command, platters of food were brought, and gourds and colorful baskets, filled with fresh berries and ripe corn, succulent venison, rabbit, and raccoon, warm cornbread, and hard, sweet maple sugar. For drinking, there were earthen cups filled with *pawcohiccora* milk made from walnuts. Smith was shown the hospitality that every guest, friend or enemy, received.

Chief Powhatan motioned to Smith to seat himself on a mat near the fire. Before he ate, he threw a piece of food into the fire, in the ritual sacrifice to Okee that all Indians performed before they ate. Then, after he had taken his food, he passed the tray to Smith.

There was little conversation during the meal. Everyone was busily eating—everyone, that is, except for Pocahontas, who was too mesmerized by the stranger's every move to eat her food. "At least he must eat food just as we do," she whispered to the woman sitting next to her. She wondered if any scraps would get caught in his beard.

Finally, all had eaten their fill and the dogs were given their bones and were chased out of the lodge. Then it was time for Chief Powhatan to speak, to ask the prisoner the questions that weighed heavily on his mind.

"Are you a king?" he asked Smith.

"No, my lord," answered Smith, wiping his beard with his sleeve. "I serve only one ruler, in a land called England."

"Why did you leave your country to come here?" the chief asked.

Smith was about to tell the truth, to say that England wanted to expand its domain, but he realized in time that this would not sit well with the powerful chieftain. Instead he replied, "We mean to conquer the enemies of our king, the Spaniards." This was not a lie. One of the reasons the English had come was to destroy the Spanish settlements in the New World.

"But if you wanted to go south where the other palefaces are, why did you come ashore on my land? And build lodges on my land?" Chief Powhatan glared at Smith; he crossed his arms across his chest.

Smith nodded thoughtfully. This was a good question—and a hard one to answer. "Because we were tired of traveling," he said, after a pause. "The sea was very rough and we were in need of fresh food."

Powhatan was not displeased by this reply. He had many other questions to ask, questions about the white man's ways that had been filling his thoughts for a long time. They spilled out in a torrent of words. "Tell me about yourself and your customs," he continued. "Why do you wear the clothes that you do? Why do you have hair upon your mouth? Do you worship the Great Spirit Okee? How powerful are your medicine men? How are you able to build such great canoes with wings? What—"

Smith answered with a smile. "I will be happy to answer all your questions," he said, "but I can do so only one at a time." He began to describe England to Powhatan, hoping to gain some time and impress the chief.

Impatiently, Opechancanough stopped Smith's recital. He wanted to tell Powhatan about the wondrous gifts the prisoner had given him. He showed the chief the compass and the watch, and Powhatan seized them eagerly, turning them over and over, holding them to his ear and his nose. He nodded his approval, and then asked about the guns that had killed one of his brother's warriors.

From this question Smith realized that their guns were the settlers' greatest protection. The Indians knew they killed and they were deathly afraid of them. He suggested to Powhatan that he come to Jamestown to see other guns for himself. "Greater ones, bigger ones, that make noise to waken the spirits," he said, waving his arms in the air.

This answer seemed to have a powerful effect on Powhatan. He began to speak rapidly to the elders sitting nearby. Then, turning back to Smith, he spoke again. But this time, his voice was no longer curious or courteous—it was cold and stern. "How soon will you leave in your canoes to go back to your own land?"

This was the question Smith had been dreading. He coughed and fingered his beard. There was danger in what he would answer, but perhaps he could soothe the Indians' fears as well.

"This land is wide, oh mighty king, with room and food enough for many tribes. We would like to join forces with you in peace, and live amongst you in harmony. In return, we will fight your enemies to the north and west, those who envy your cornfields and your hunting grounds. Let us be friends and allies, Chief Powhatan. This land pleases us and we would like to stay."

Smith could not read Powhatan's expression. It was the first time a white man had explained his presence in the land to an Indian. Suddenly, a great uproar arose in the crowd. There was much shouting back and forth, and Powhatan consulted with several of his powerful allies. Smith knew that his fate was being decided, but the Indians spoke too rapidly for him to make out what it would be. Finally, Powhatan waved his hand for silence and issued a command.

It was the death sentence. Every eye was now turned toward Smith. He smiled, however, as if they had brought him good news. With his customary courage, he believed that if his death could save the colony, it would be welcome. It was not that he did not love life, but he was one of those souls to whom a cause, or a quest, is dearer than life. And because of its very weakness, its dependence upon him, the colony had become a child he must protect at all costs.

Even if Pocahontas could have read John Smith's thoughts, she could not have understood them. But as she listened to her father's verdict, she felt the same dizzyness as when Claw-of-the-Eagle had almost been killed, before old Wansutis saved him and adopted him into the tribe.

When she saw the Englishman smile, she knew him to be a brave man and she felt a great sorrow. She did not want him to die. She felt sorrow for herself, as well. The stranger could have told her many tales of new lands and strange people—exciting stories far more interesting than those she had already heard many times over. How eagerly she would have listened to him! Her father was a wise leader and she knew he had every reason to fear the presence of the white man in his land. But why must he kill this leader? Why not keep him a prisoner and learn the secrets of his white tribe's powerful medicine?

But there seemed nothing Pocahontas could do. She saw that the braves had lost no time in obeying the command given them. They were dragging in the two great stones that had not been used for many moons. These were set in the open space facing Powhatan, and Pocahontas knew exactly what was to follow.

Was there any possibility of escape? John Smith asked himself.

He would gladly have fired his pistol at Powhatan and, in the ensuing confusion, rushed through the crowd and out of the lodge. But, alas, his gun was empty. No use struggling, he thought. He did not want to meet his death as a coward.

So, when two young braves seized him at Powhatan's signal, he made no resistance. They threw him down on the ground, then lifted his head up on the stones, while another brave, holding a stone hatchet in his hand, strode forward and stood next to his undefended head.

Well, John Smith thought, my life is over. I have traveled many a mile to come to this end. What will happen to Jamestown now? At least I did not fail them. I am glad of that now.

He saw Powhatan lean forward and give a sign. The war-painted face of his executioner held no expression as he raised the tomahawk. Smith watched its quick descent and instinctively closed his eyes.

But the tomahawk did *not* descend. After what seemed an eternity of suspense, Smith opened his eyes again to see what had delayed it. The brave still held the tomahawk poised in the air. He was gazing impatiently at Powhatan, at whose feet knelt the young girl Smith had noticed on entering the village. He could see that the child was pleading for his life. But why?

But Powhatan would not listen to his daughter's pleading and he angrily ordered her away. His voice was terrifying, and his wives, fearing that he would hurt Pocahontas, pulled her away from him. Powhatan nodded again to the executioner to obey his command.

Suddenly, with a quick leap, Pocahontas flung herself across Smith's body, took his head in her arms, and laid her own head down against his. The tomahawk had stopped but a feather's breadth from her black hair, so close that the Indian who held it could scarcely breathe for fear it might have injured the daughter of Chief Powhatan.

For a moment, it looked as if Powhatan, furious at such disobedience, was about to order the blow to fall on both heads. There was complete silence among the observers, and those at the back of the lodge pushed forward so they would not miss what was to come. Then Powhatan spoke. "Rise, Matoaka!" he thundered. "Do not dare to interfere with my justice!"

"No, Father," cried Pocahontas, lifting her head while her arms still lay protectively around Smith's neck. "I claim this man from you. Just as Wansutis adopted Claw-of-the-Eagle, so I will adopt this paleface into our tribe."

Everyone began to talk at once.

"She wants such a foolish thing!"

"She has the right."

"If he lives, how can we be safe?"

"But since our first forefathers lived on this land, our women have been allowed to adopt someone into the tribe. . . ."

"Yes, but a paleface!"

Powhatan raised his hand and the chattering stopped at once. He spoke sternly. "Do you claim him in true earnestness, Matoaka?"

"Yes, Father," she answered. "I claim him with full knowledge of my heart and mind. Do not slay him. Let him live among us. He can make hatchets for you, and bells and beads and copper necklaces for me. Remember the pact we made with your robe?" Pocahontas reached out and touched the pattern she had so lovingly and painstakingly stitched. "You are wearing it now, to remind you of your love for me and your promise to grant me whatever I might wish."

Powhatan nodded. "I remember." He paused and sighed. "So be it," he finally said.

Pocahontas rose to her feet and, taking Smith by the hand, pulled him up. He got clumsily to his feet, dazed by his sudden deliverance, and not understanding in the least how it had come about.

CHAPTER 9

SMITH'S JAILER

On the following morning, Claw-of-the-Eagle found Pocahontas sitting outside the lodge housing John Smith.

He quickly looked around. "What are you doing here all alone?" he asked. "Where are the guards?"

Pocahontas yawned and smiled up at Claw-of-the-Eagle. "Do not worry. I sent the guards away as soon as the Sun returned to us."

Claw-of-the-Eagle looked at her with astonishment. He shook his head.

"It is true," Pocahontas laughed. "I can take care of him myself during the day."

Claw-of-the-Eagle was very curious about the Englishman. He leaned down to Pocahontas and whispered, "Have you seen him yet? What is he like? How does he look? What does he say?"

"Shhh!" Pocahontas put her finger to her lips. "He still sleeps. I just looked between the bark coverings and saw him lying there with his eyes closed, wearing his strange garments." She sighed and sifted some earth through her hands. "I wish he would wake up! There are so many questions I would like to ask him."

"Let me see him. Please," Claw-of-the-Eagle pleaded.

Pocahontas nodded and motioned graciously toward the lodge. It made her feel generous to grant favors just as her father did. Indeed, Powhatan sometimes smiled when he saw how much her manner of bestowing them resembled his.

Using the same caution as when he crept after a deer in the thicket, Claw-of-the-Eagle silently crawled through the lodge opening on his hands and knees. He moved slowly toward the softly snoring Englishman, stopping to stare when he was only a few feet away.

Lying flat on his stomach, the boy gazed at the Englishman. He had heard the details of his rescue within the ceremonial lodge many times during the night, and many were the opinions he heard about the event. Some looked on Chief Powhatan's decision as a danger to them all, but others scoffed at the idea that palefaces were to be feared by brave Indian warriors. However, Claw-of-the-Eagle did not waver in *his* belief that every one of the white strangers should be killed—and quickly. His loyalty to his adopted tribe was as great as if his own forefathers had sat around its council fires. As much as he liked Pocahontas, Claw-of-the-Eagle was sorry that she had persuaded her father to save the life of the first paleface to have fallen into his hands. He believed that Chief Powhatan himself now regretted that he had been swayed by his affection for his daughter, and that he had allowed her to invoke the ancient custom. He thought that the chief would now gladly see his enemy dead so that this would serve as a warning to his fellow interlopers of the fate that awaited them all.

It was then that the thought occurred to him that he,

Claw-of-the-Eagle, could make this happen! Powhatan would never think to punish the doer of the deed.

Resolved to do this thing, the boy crept nearer to the sleeping man, while loosening the knife in his belt. There was no sound inside the lodge but he could faintly hear Pocahontas singing outside.

But then something, some instinctual feeling of danger, roused the Englishman. Through his half-closed lids, he could barely distinguish the slowly advancing body in the gloom. When the boy was close enough to touch him, Smith opened his eyes wide. He did not move, he did not cry out, even though he saw the knife in the boy's hand. He fixed his gaze sternly on the boy's face. Claw-of-the-Eagle tried to strike, but with those fearless eyes upon him, he could not move his arm.

Slowly, as he had come, he returned to the entrance, unable to turn his gaze from the man who watched him. It was only when he was out in the air again that Claw-of-the-Eagle felt he could take a long breath.

"He is a good sleeper" was all he said to Pocahontas.

"And doubtless he is as good an eater and will be hungry when he wakes," she answered. "Will you stop at my lodge, Claw-of-the-Eagle, and ask them to bring some food for him?"

The boy did as she asked, and soon some women arrived carrying bread and meat. They peered eagerly through the crack between the bark coverings until Pocahontas sent them away. Hearing a noise within the lodge, she assumed that Smith was awake. She was about to take him the food, when he stepped outside.

Smith was astonished to see the sentinel they had set to guard him. He had expected to find his unexpected guest waiting outside for another chance at his life, and he had thought to hasten the moment. But he knew immediately that this young maiden was as good a jailer as a hundred braves. If Smith so much as attempted an escape back to Jamestown, her outcry would bring the entire village running. He recognized his savior of the day before and bowed low, a bow meant for the princess and protector. Though this European gesture was strange to her, Pocahontas felt sure it was intended as an honor and she received it gravely and graciously.

"Here is food for you, White Chief," she said, placing the bowls on a mat she had spread on the ground. "Sit and eat."

"Thank you," Smith answered, "but first I must speak with you." He knelt down besides Pocahontas and gazed at her. "I have no words in your language, little Princess, to thank you for your great gift, and though my words are as plentiful as grains of sand, they are still too few to offer you."

"Gifts made to chiefs," she answered with her father's dignity, gazing directly back at Smith, "are never gifts. They are a privilege and I am privileged to have bestowed a gift upon you, White Chief."

Smith could not help smiling at such grandiose language from one so young.

"But," she continued, clasping her arms around her knees, "I am pleased by your thanks. You are very welcome."

Pocahontas then put aside her grown-up airs and showed herself the exuberant and curious child that she in fact was. She gently fingered the sleeve of Smith's jacket, stained by mud and torn by thorns.

"It is good English cloth," he remarked, "to have withstood such abuse, and I bless the sheep on whose backs it grew."

"Sheep? What kind of beasts are those?" she asked, and Smith tried to explain what sheep looked like and how their wool was used.

But Pocahontas interrupted him. There was too much to know

to dwell on any one subject—and she had other, more personal questions on her mind. "Did your wife make your coat?" she asked, blushing at her own boldness.

"I have no wife, little Princess," answered Smith.

"I am glad," she said, sighing.

Smith smiled. "And why are you glad?"

Pocahontas spread her fingers through the soil. "I do not know." Her brow wrinkled as she tried to understand her own feelings. "Perhaps it is because you will not miss her and so try to leave us."

"But I must leave here soon, Princess," he said, biting into a piece of warm bread. "My people at Jamestown are waiting for me." Smith looked intently at Pocahontas, trying to read her thoughts. He hoped to discover Powhatan's intentions toward him. As grateful as he was to the Princess, now that his life had been saved his only thought was for freedom.

"You shall not go," Pocahontas cried, jumping up. "You belong to me, and it is my wish to keep you here so that you may tell me tales of the world beyond the sunrise. You cannot go. I will not let you!"

"So be it," said Smith in a flat tone. Inside, he was sick with grief. His colleagues at Jamestown were ill. They were starving— and now, believing that Smith must be dead, they were certainly hopeless as well.

Smith knew that the only thing he could do was bide his time. He hoped to be able to send a message to Jamestown soon. In the meantime, it made sense to make friends with his captors—especially his little savior, Pocahontas.

Since Smith did not oppose her, Pocahontas quieted and sat back beside him. Already an audience crowded around them, watching the paleface eat. Smith had learned quickly in captivity that the Indians valued a calm, impassive manner, so he ate without hurry—and as if he were completely alone. He cut off bits of venison with his knife and chewed them very slowly. But one boy could not contain his curiosity. He slipped in front of the crowd and jerked Smith's beard. Pocahontas immediately ordered him away.

"Do not be angry," she said to Smith. "He only wanted to find out if your beard was real."

Pocahontas would not say so, but she shared the boy's curiosity about the beard. Perhaps, she thought, it was some kind of decoration Smith put on when he set out on the warpath, just as her people dressed themselves on special occasions in painted masks.

Smith tugged at his beard with both hands, smiling, and his audience laughed. They could appreciate a joke, it seemed, and he was glad to see that they were friendly toward him—if only for the moment.

One of the older men in the crowd pointed to the pocket in Smith's vest and asked what he had in it. His compass and watch were gone, but Smith reached into its depths hoping to find something he had forgotten which might interest them. He was in luck! Smith brought out a pencil and a small notebook. He wrote a few words and handed the notebook to Pocahontas, telling her that the words were powerful medicine. "If someone could carry them to Jamestown they would speak to my people and they would hear there what I have said here at Werowocomoco."

Pocahontas shook her head—as did most of the audience. The stranger might do many wonderful things, but this trick was beyond the power of even the greatest magician.

Smith, however, refused to give up. He was determined to press the point of his eventual return to Jamestown. "It is possible for me, Princess, to do even greater magic, if you would let me go to Jamestown. You can come with me."

"No!" she repeated angrily. "You will never go there again. You are mine and you must obey me!" She looked out at the crowd and defiantly crossed her arms over her chest.

The audience shouted its agreement, confirming Smith's suspicions that his fate, unbelievable as it seemed, had been placed in the hands of this young girl. He sighed. There was nothing to do but answer the countless questions being shouted to him from the crowd.

In turn, he questioned the Indians about their harvests, their methods of planting and harvesting corn—but the crowd plainly showed that they liked asking him questions much more than answering his.

As the day advanced, the crowd began to dwindle. Everyone knew that the prisoner would not be leaving Werowocomoco and there was much to do in the village. Some of the boys had become restless and had left to play games. Soon only Pocahontas was left.

Smith glanced around to see what his chances for a sudden escape might be, but the sight of some braves sharpening their arrowheads not more than a hundred feet away made him think again. He settled down once more and tried to be patient.

"Tell me, White Chief," said Pocahontas, as she lighted a pipe she had filled with tobacco and passed it to Smith. "Tell me about yourself and your people. Are you really like us? Do you die as we do, or can your medicine keep you alive forever? Can you change yourself into an animal? Can you fly through the air? Tell me, tell me!" Pocahontas clapped her hands with excitement.

Smith looked at her again. He had never met anyone whose spirit was more full of life. In her enthusiasm, he recognized his own love of adventure and the desire to explore new lands. She could not sail across the ocean in search of them as he had done.

All went about their business as if Smith
were no longer there
Page 82

"I will lead the princess."
Page 96

Instead, he realized, *he* was her great adventure, a living book of strange tales that would fire her imagination.

This pleased John Smith. He did love to tell of his adventures across many lands and many seas. The sun was warm and pleasant on his face; a breeze ruffled his collar. The tobacco, which he learned how to smoke only since capture, soothed his spirits, and as he gazed around the village, he knew he was in no immediate danger. He smiled at the bright-eyed Pocahontas and began to talk.

Although he was hampered by his limited vocabulary in the Powhatan language, Smith was able to convey the spirit and the colorful details of his travels, from the exotic bazaars of Turkey to his life in green and beautiful England. He told Pocahontas about the young Persian girl, very much like Pocahontas herself, who had kept him in her room and had treated him in the same manner as her pet tiger! Luckily, he had escaped one moonlit night and had hidden for weeks in a golden mosque. He described his arduous journey across the water, his past service to the red-haired Queen Elizabeth, and to the present monarch, King James. Pocahontas watched him, fascinated as he made up for his lack of vocabulary with elaborate hand gestures and pantomimes.

"And then, Princess—"

"Please," Pocahontas interrupted him, "call me Pocahontas, as my people do. Let us always be friends."

Smith smiled. He liked this young girl who was so mature for a thirteen-year-old. He admired her courage and her enthusiasm.

"That I will agree to . . . Pocahontas."

And he continued his tales as the sun traveled across the sky.

CHAPTER 10

The Lodge in the Woods

The daylight had almost faded from the sky and the air became cooler. The crickets had begun their evening call. All too soon, it was time for Pocahontas to leave John Smith for her evening meal. But she did not return to say good-night. In fact, Smith did not have a private conversation with her again. The next day and for three days after, Pocahontas came to see him, but she was always accompanied by others: her friends, her sister, tribal wives, curious toddlers. She would smile at him, give him his meal of meat, maize, and fruit, and leave.

Pocahontas was not the only one who seemed to lose interest in the white stranger. When he had first arrived at Werowocomoco everyone had come to gaze at him. Wise chieftains from other tribes came to speak with him. But now, all went about their business, as if Smith were no longer there. The women tanned hides and cut them into strips for sewing; they sewed beads on skirts and tunics; they cooked meals and tended the fires. The men entered and left the village, carrying deer and rabbits and corn and other food plants for storage. The children, too, ignored Smith; they went back to their games and their pet dogs. Smith actually missed the way they used to peer into his lodge, half afraid and half excited, their eyes filled with wonder and glee.

On the surface, it seemed that Smith had been accepted as a member of the Powhatan tribe, as Pocahontas had promised. But Smith was wary. He was being ignored too much. And something seemed to be happening in the long lodge where he had almost lost his life. He saw braves and elders gathering around, talking and gesturing. They were too far away for him to hear, but they made him feel afraid. He had no idea what the future would bring. He didn't know if he would ever see Jamestown again.

On the third day of his captivity, Smith saw Pocahontas leave her lodge. He sat up, a smile on his face. He had missed her exuberant, enthusiastic presence. But Pocahontas went right by him; she didn't even look his way. She ran to the wigwams at the edge of the forest, looking for old Wansutis.

Smith watched until he lost sight of her. He sighed and decided to take a nap in the warm sun.

Although it seemed that Pocahontas had forgotten him, John Smith was, however, very much on the girl's mind. In fact, her purpose in seeking out old Wansutis was to find a way to bewitch Smith into forgetting about Jamestown, England, and his very roots.

Claw-of-the-Eagle was surprised to see Pocahontas in that part of the woods. The princess, and the others in the tribe, feared his adoptive mother, who they believed was a witch. No one wished to cross her for fear of retaliation. The stories about her flourished: how she made this one an owl, that one a stone, and yet another a fish in the seas far to the south.

"Pocahontas!" he shouted. "Wait."

The young princess turned. "Claw-of-the-Eagle," she said as she stopped to wait. "Is Wansutis at home?"

"Yes," he replied, walking beside her toward his lodge. Claw-of-the-Eagle wanted very much to discover what Pocahontas wanted from his mother, but he dared not ask a princess about her business.

Pocahontas took a deep breath and tried not to think about what it would be like to be a fish in the ocean or an owl that never blinked the whole night through.

Claw-of-the-Eagle entered his mother's lodge behind Pocahontas. In order to stay and hear what it was Pocahontas wanted, he sat quietly pretending to string his bows.

"Wansutis," Pocahontas began, standing in the entrance. The old woman sat smoking in the darkest part of the lodge; Pocahontas could not see her eyes. She swallowed and spoke again. "Wansutis," she repeated, "you have knowledge of all the herbs of the fields and the forests, those that harm and those that help. Is this not so?"

The old woman looked up, a smile upon her wrinkled lips. "Ah!" she said. "So Princess Pocahontas comes to old Wansutis for a love potion."

"No!" the girl cried angrily, moving into the lodge. "Not so. I need something different—herbs that will make a person forget."

"It's the same herb for both," snapped Wansutis. "And for whom will you brew it? Your adopted son, perhaps—you who are too young to be a wife and too young to have a son? I have no such herb, Princess. And if I had, do you not think that I would have given it to Claw-of-the-Eagle? Speak to her, my son. Tell her if it is so that a person can ever forget."

Pocahontas turned a questioning glance at the young brave, who coughed self-consciously and answered, "My thoughts are great and speedy travelers, Pocahontas. They take long journeys back to my father's and mother's people. They wander old trails in the forests and they meet old friends by the side of burned-out campfires. Yet, like weary hunters who have been seeking game all day, they return at night in gratitude to Wansutis and her lodge." Claw-of-the-Eagle paused and smiled at his adoptive mother. He put down his bow.

"Wansutis has not tried to stop my thoughts from traveling old trails, nor has she tied my feet to her wigwam pole to keep my thoughts from straying."

"And if she had not left you free to think?" queried Pocahontas, her brow furrowed. "What would you have done?"

"I do not know, Princess," the boy answered after a pause. "If my father and mother were still alive, I would have sought to return to them—even if your father had surrounded the village with guards. But they are no more, and our distant wigwam is empty. So my heart finds rest in a new home and I gladly share my life with my new mother."

"Is it that hard to forget old ways?" Pocahontas wondered aloud. "It seems to me that each day among strangers would be the beginning of a new life, and that it would be exciting not to know what would come to pass before nightfall."

She paused, looking eagerly at both the old woman and the boy, her eyes now used to the darkness. "Why should this pale-face desire to return to an island where they are sick and starving while here he finds food and comfort?"

"Wait until you yourself are among strangers far from your own people," snapped Wansutis sternly. Then she turned her back on the young people and began to mutter.

"So you have no drink of forgetfulness to give me?" Pocahontas asked with a sigh. She hesitated one last time at the entrance to the lodge. But the old woman did not answer; the smoke from her pipe filled the air. Pocahontas walked slowly away while Claw-of-the-Eagle, bow in hand, gazed after her.

It had grown dark and John Smith, his legs cramped from sitting, stretched himself out by the fire in his lodge. He added some twigs, so that the embers which had smoldered all day now blazed up brightly. The cheerful crackling was welcome; it reminded him of his English home. The fire was not only a companion, but a protection as well. He might be seized and put to death while it burned, but at least he would be able to see his enemies by its light as they came at him.

Smith thought about Pocahontas. He missed her. She was not only the freest, boldest, and brightest person he had ever met, but her presence, like the fire, also meant protection. Without her, he worried for his own safety. Anything could happen.

His thoughts were disturbed by the entrance of two Indians. "We have come at Chief Powhatan's bidding," they said. "We are to take you to his lodge in the wood."

It seemed as if his worst fears were to be realized—but Smith was not afraid. At least the monotony of his captivity would be broken. He quickly rose and followed the men through the village, where from each wigwam a ghostly curl of smoke rose toward the dark sky. Through the hide coverings, Smith could see families silhouetted by the fires as they sat and ate their evening meals before lying down to sleep. Soon the trio had left the peaceful village for the forest, where they approached and then entered a lodge as big as the one in which Smith had first faced Chief Powhatan.

This lodge, however, was arranged differently. It was divided into two sections separated by dark hanging mats that permitted no light to pass through. Smith was ushered into the smaller section and, after stirring up the fire and throwing on fresh logs, the Indians left him. Smith was alone.

It did not take long for Smith to realize that there were others in the lodge. He heard the sounds of muffled feet on the other side of the hanging mats. He heard what he believed to be a group of people settling down on the earth. Then, after a short silence, he heard a lone voice begin to chant in low tones. He could not understand the words, but he heard the group rise and begin to move rhythmically in what he thought must a dance. Someone shook a rattle in time to the muffled feet and the voices which were now raised in unison.

The ground shook. The voices grew louder. The rattle shook faster, and faster still. Smith tried desperately to see what was behind the mat, but it was no use. He was certain that the ceremony being enacted on the other side was a preamble to his approaching death, in which the dancers rejoiced in his coming end.

Smith sighed deeply and sank to the ground. Perhaps Chief Powhatan had only pretended to grant his daughter's request. Or perhaps Pocahontas had changed her mind. Whatever the reason, Smith knew that he would soon be killed. He prayed for swift death.

The noise grew louder and more frightening. Then Smith noticed that the bottom corner of the mat wavered and bulged. Suddenly, the mat was lifted and a tall, broad Indian came dancing in, his body painted in bold red dye, his face covered by a ferocious mask, and his head covered with an elaborate headdress made of feathers, shells, and beads. Although the mask hid his features, Smith recognized the build and the stance of Chief Powhatan himself.

Behind Powhatan came other braves and chieftains, two hundred in all, chanting and dancing around the fire. Smith began to pray again in earnest, but, to his astonishment, no tomahawk fell, no arrow pierced his skin. Then, barely able to believe his ears, Smith thought he heard the word for friend.

There it was again: friend. Suddenly, the chanting and the dancing stopped. The medicine man dropped his rattle. Powhatan took off his mask and approached Smith. He nodded to the white man.

"Have no fear, my son. We have not come to harm you. In this sacred ritual we have spoken to our god, Okee, proclaiming our friendship with you. From this moment forward, your tribe and ours are one. You are no longer a prisoner. You are free to come and go as is any brave. You may now go back to your island, if you wish."

Smith bowed to the great chieftain. He shook his head to clear it. He hardly believed what he was hearing.

"We have but one request," continued Powhatan. "We ask that when you return to your people, you send me two of your great guns that spit fire and death, so that my name will be more powerful than that of my enemies. I would also like to have one of your grindstones so that we may grind our corn with more ease. In return, you will always have a place in my tribe. You will always be my brother."

The more Powhatan talked, the more difficult it was for Smith not to betray his surprise. First came the relief at learning that he was not to be killed immediately—and then the wonderful news that he was free to return to Jamestown. And if Chief Powhatan and his people had sworn friendship to him, it would mean also that the colony would be saved.

Smith longed to know what had brought about this unexpected change in his fate, but he could not ask. He could only guess that Powhatan's desire for English goods had overpowered his fear—and that the Indians were indeed a peaceful people who would gladly share their land.

In as stately a manner as he could muster, Smith spoke of his gratitude. "I thank you, great Powhatan, for your words of kindness and your good news. In truth, if you will be a father to me, I will be a son to you, and there shall be peace between Werowocomoco and Jamestown. If you will send men to show me the way home, and also provisions for my people, I promise that they will return with the gifts you request."

Powhatan turned and spoke. Twelve men stepped forward and announced themselves ready to accompany the paleface. Smith could hardly believe that he was free to leave that night. He was so eager to be off that he barely said farewell. He did not even think to search out Pocahontas to say good-bye.

The men set off through the forest. Along its edge were the clearings where corn grew in summer. Soon the trees were close upon one another and it seemed to Smith that there was no path between them. But his guides strode quickly along without hesitation. Although the night was dark and the forest crowded, the Indians easily found their way along the invisible path.

Six of the Indians walked in front of Smith and six behind. No one spoke. There were only the faint sounds of the Englishman's boots and his occasional stumbling against unseen trunks or rocks to break the silence. There was little chance that an enemy would come so near Chief Powhatan's camp, but the Indians observed their usual caution nevertheless.

For John Smith, there was something ghostly about this night excursion, through unknown country, with unknown men. He could not help but wonder whether he had understood correctly all that Powhatan had said, or if he dared believe that he had meant what he said—or whether he really planned to kill him in the wilderness away from any voice that could speak in his defense. And then there was the possibility that even though Powhatan himself was acting in good faith, the tribal chiefs might have chosen to act on their own to put an end to the white man whose comings and goings were beyond their understanding. In spite of these doubts, Smith walked on, trying to appear as unafraid as if he were strolling in the garden of his English home.

The call of some animal, a wildcat perhaps, brought the little company to a standstill, and a huddled consultation. Smith knew the sound could have come from some beast, but it could also be the call of a lurking enemy—or even a signal from Powhatan to kill him now!

If it was a signal, it boded ill for Smith and he needed quickly to form a strategy. Smith clasped a stone knife he had managed to secrete at Werowocomoco. He could not overhear what his Indian companions were saying, but they seemed to be arguing. Suddenly, they appeared to come to some decision and they started off once again.

Though the forest was dark and dense, Smith's eyes had grown more accustomed to the blackness and he began to distinguish between the various shades of darkness. Once or twice, he thought he saw another figure among the trees, moving and halting in concert with his group. But when he looked fixedly, Smith could see nothing but the trunk of some huge tree or other.

On and on they went, hooted at by owls and sung to by whippoorwills, crossing streams over log bridges, wading through others where cold water splashed up at their faces.

At last, the blackness faded to gray, and Smith could make out the fingers of his hand. Dawn was near. Why, wondered the Englishman, did their followers delay striking for so long? If they meant to kill him, he hoped it would happen quickly. The phantom "wildcat" that had accompanied them had to act soon.

Suddenly the landscape ahead of them seemed to grow wider

and lighter. The trees were now farther apart and the figures of the men themselves were more visible. What was it that he saw in front of him, beyond the forest? Could it be. . . .

"Jamestown!" he cried out in English. "Jamestown! Yonder is Jamestown! God be praised!"

The Indians gathered around him and questioned him eagerly. Would he give all of them gifts? Would they receive the guns and grindstone to carry back to Powhatan?

As they stood in a tight huddle, a young man ran up behind them. The Indians turned.

"Claw-of-the-Eagle!" they exclaimed.

Without a word, the boy placed a necklace of white shells in the hands of the astonished Smith. Smith remembered that Pocahontas had worn it when they had talked that first night.

"Princess Pocahontas sends greetings," Claw-of-the-Eagle said, "and bids you farewell now that she has seen you safely to your people." The young Indian was scowling, in contrast to the kind words that came from his lips.

And, at that moment, John Smith knew that Pocahontas had been the phantom "wildcat" who had accompanied them on their trek through the forest. And he also knew beyond a shadow of a doubt that if death had been near him that night, it was Pocahontas who had saved him once again.

CHAPTER 11

Pocahontas Visits Jamestown

Smith's heart felt full at the sight of the familiar huts and the sturdy fort before him; their outlines grew more and more distinct as the sun rose higher.

He answered the hail from a disbelieving sentry who, once he had convinced himself that his eyes and ears did not betray him, ran to Smith and clasped his hands.

"Captain," he exclaimed, "it is indeed a happy day that brings you back to us."

Smith made an introduction between the sentry and his Indian guides. "We have brought the White Chief safely back to his tribe," one of them said. "Now you must make good your promise to give us the guns and the grindstone."

Smith smiled. "You will receive that and more. I give you my word."

As the group entered the fort, the Indians eyed the place with great curiosity; Smith looked around with gratitude and relief.

92

Although the fortress itself was absolutely worthless by military standards—it was unable to withstand an attack of heavy guns—the Indians found it imposing. They had never seen anything built quite like it, from the mortar between the logs, to the huge trunks from which the high tower was constructed.

Smith looked up and removed his hat in deference to the English flag that waved over the towering scaffold. The Indians, too, bowed their heads in respect. When one of the Englishmen granted Smith's request to fire a cannon, the Indians fell to the ground, sure that the sound would kill them.

After a few moments, they realized they were unhurt and they rose. They saw that the white man's magic was powerful indeed —which was just what Smith had intended, especially since their fort was, in reality, so vulnerable.

"Guns are not playthings," cautioned Smith. "We will show you how to use them before you take them back to your tribe. Otherwise, you will injure yourselves."

The Indians nodded, still trembling from the cannon's roar They were staring at the men and women who had come out of their homes at the sound of the gun. They looked thin and pale. They were weak and starving. They looked hungrily at the baskets of food the Indians carried, more intent on nourishment than on welcoming home their Captain Smith.

And, indeed, there were those who were not pleased to see him, friends of President Wingfield who were jealous of Smith and who did not want him to have much power. They turned their backs when Smith walked by, merely nodding at him.

President Wingfield approached from the door of the government house. "Welcome back, Smith," he said, looking him up and down. "I see you are none the worse for wear." He licked his lips on seeing the baskets the Indians carried. "Indeed, it is nice to know you were so well cared for during your captivity." He paused and then said sternly, "It is a shame that the men who left with you did not fare as well. I understand that they are dead."

Smith would not be cowed by Wingfield. He doffed his hat not to the man, but out of respect for his office. "If they had followed my orders," he replied, "they would be standing with me now. And, as you can see, I have brought food to cure the hunger that has besieged us for months. I do believe that takes precedence." Smith gestured toward the baskets and motioned the Indians to follow him to the storehouse.

"I expect a full report from you, Captain Smith," Wingfield called coldly after Smith's retreating back. "Particulary with regard to your missing men." Smith ignored him as he beckoned the Indians inside the storehouse. They emptied the baskets of corn, venison, beans, and cranberries, and refilled them with beads, iron pots, shiny brass kettles, steel knives, and colorful cloth. Smith also helped them hoist a grindstone onto a makeshift wagon.

Before the Indians left to return home, Smith promised that he would show them at another time how to use a gun. He said to them in their own tongue, "Ask Pocahontas to bring two baskets and I will fill them with white beads so that she can make another necklace. Ask her to come soon."

After the Indians had gone, Smith's friends and colleagues gave him the news of the colony. Many of the settlers, friend and foe alike, had died of starvation, from the harshness of their environment, from fever. "This is not a friendly land, Captain Smith," said a wan, gaunt man.

But Smith had brought life back to the colony. He had brought not only provisions to last a long while, but also the farming methods he had learned from the Indians. And, most of all, he had brought them renewed hope and confidence.

Soon the men were following his robust lead, felling trees, planting seeds, and laying bricks for new lodgings. President Wingfield's threats came to naught and life in Jamestown slowly grew better.

Throughout the following weeks and months, Smith thought often of Pocahontas. He hoped she would visit someday soon.

That day did not come until many months later. It was deep winter, when the snow had fallen often and heavily and food was once again scarce.

Smith and several other men were gathered around a bonfire, cooking some dried sturgeon they would have to share. He was showing them a rough parchment chart on which he had drawn a plan, showing how he envisioned the future growth of Jamestown, when suddenly everyone grew quiet. Smith noticed the silence and looked up. There, in front of him, was Claw-of-the-Eagle, the boy who had once tried to kill him and who later had given him the necklace and message from Pocahontas.

Claw-of-the-Eagle still did not trust Smith, or any of the pale-faces. But he was loyal to his princess. He took a deep breath and began to speak. "Chief of the white men, Princess Pocahontas sent me to inform you that she has come to visit. She and her friends await you by the fort."

"She is most welcome," Smith said delightedly. He called out to his comrades. "Come with me to receive the daughter of Chief Powhatan. She is the young girl who saved me at the risk of her own life."

The colonists needed no urging. They were most curious to see what an Indian princess looked like, especially the one who had saved their hero.

When Smith caught sight of Pocahontas, his face broke into a smile. He stretched out his hands to her in welcome.

"Ah! Little friend," he said with delight. "I owe you so much,

Pocahontas—my life, my freedom, my return home, and now this pleasure!"

Pocahontas merely smiled. Smith then turned, gesturing toward the men who had followed him. "These are my comrades, Princess, and they too would thank you if they could speak your language."

The men swept off their hats and bowed to the princess. Pocahontas acknowledged their courtesy with great dignity.

"Let us show these guests our town," urged Smith, "even though it lacks palaces and bazaars filled with color and bright goods. I will lead the princess." He turned to his men. "You take care of the young brave and her other friends."

As they walked along the path from the fort to Jamestown's single street, Smith said to Pocahontas, "Tell me, my gentle jailer, do you know why your father set me free? I have wondered every day since then, and I cannot understand." Smith took her elbow and guided Pocahontas through the muddy grooves made by wagons and heavy feet. "I thought it was perhaps the promise of guns and presents, but I do not believe that would have been enough for a complete change of mind." He looked at her. "It was your doing, was it not?"

"Yes," whispered Pocahontas, her attention momentarily diverted from the town. She looked at Smith. "I began to feel sorry that you were so far from your people. I knew that you could never forget them, so I pleaded with my father until he finally relented. I told him that your friendship would prove a help to us, a high tide that covers sharp rocks over which we could safely ride."

Smith nodded. He gazed at Pocahontas with new respect. She was wise beyond her years. "And the songs and dances in the woods? What of those, Pocahontas?"

"It was a ceremonial dance to initiate you into our tribe. You and my father are now united forever. You are his son and I am your sister." Pocahontas smiled, then once again stared at the buildings and wagons and fences around her.

But Smith was insistent. "One last question, Princess." He stopped and placed his hands over those of Pocahontas. "Was it you in the woods the night I was guided home? Did you still fear for my safety even though your father had given his word?"

Pocahontas turned away and refused to answer.

Smith's whisper was filled with feeling. "I can never repay you for all that you have done for me, little sister."

Pocahontas turned now to face Smith. She was about to reply when she was distracted by a sight that broke her serious mood and caused her to laugh and laugh. Two men had been rolling a barrel of flour from the storehouse when it slipped and rolled against another who had been standing with his back to the barrel. It caught him behind his shins and sent him sprawling, covered in white. It looked so funny and harmless that Pocahontas could not contain her mirth. But her laughter ceased when she saw that the man did not rise again.

"Why does he not get up?" asked Pocahontas. "He cannot be badly hurt. It was such a light blow."

Smith sighed. "I fear it is because he is weak from hunger," he answered gravely.

"Why? Has he not enough to eat?" asked the girl in wide-eyed wonder. And then she understood. "You do not have enough food, do you?" She stamped her moccasined feet. "None of you!"

Smith nodded. "It is true, little sister, our stores are short. If a ship does not come soon from England with supplies, I fear for our lives."

"No!" she cried emphatically, shaking her head until her long, beaded and feathered braids swung to and fro. "You shall not starve while there is plenty at Werowocomoco. This very night I will myself send provisions to you." Pocahontas paused and sighed deeply. "It hurts me here," she said, laying her hand on her heart, "to think that you are suffering."

Just then President Wingfield and several officers of the Council approached the two. They had heard the news of Pocahontas's visit and they knew that the presence of the best-loved daughter of a powerful Indian chieftain was an important event. As they came near, they wondered what they would find. Their vague expectations that they would meet with some exotic form of royalty led them to think they would come face to face with one of royal bearing, magnificently dressed. So they were quite taken aback to find, instead, a slim young girl whose garments were meager and unimpressive. She wore no royal purple, no jewel-studded crown, and yet there was something about her that proved unmistakably that she was a princess after all. She carried herself with a dignity that was both confident and regal. It seemed, suddenly, as if *their* best starched collars and ruffs were inadequate.

Pocahontas watched them, carefully concealing her amazement at their strange appearance. She heard their words of welcome and answered them through her interpreter, John Smith. But all the while she was studying every detail of their dress and bearing.

"We must give her gifts," suggested one of the councilmen as if this were an idea that had come to no one else. He sent a servant to fetch some of the trinkets which they had brought for bartering.

Pocahontas clapped her hands in delight as Smith placed a long chain of white and blue beads over her head. Her pleasure was even greater when he held up a little mirror and she saw her face for the first time reflected in something that was not a forest pool.

"Is that, too, for me?" she asked eagerly, clasping the mirror to her breast when it was placed in her hand. She peered into it, from one side and the other, making new acquaintance with her own features.

While the councilmen distributed presents to the other Indians, Smith hurried off to his own house. After hunting through his chest, he found a silver bracelet which he took outside and slipped onto Pocahontas's arm. "This is to remind Pocahontas always that she is my sister and that I am her brother."

Pocahontas was deeply touched—and filled with so many new sensations that she found herself overwhelmed. She wished to be by herself, to think about all she had seen, to look at her new belongings one by one. She felt now that she must leave as soon as possible.

"I must return to my father's lodge," she said, and she did not speak again until they had reached the fort. As the Indians began their homeward trek through the forest, Pocahontas turned back to wave at Smith. "Brother, I will not forget my promise," she called out to him. "Tonight, I will send you food. I am very pleased with your strange town and I will come again. Farewell."

CHAPTER 12

POWHATAN'S AMBASSADOR

Pocahontas was true to her word. That same night, after she had told Powhatan about the strange place called Jamestown and showed him her treasures, she and her friends filled basket upon basket with corn, dried venison, bear meat, and dried cranberries. She sent the provisions off with the swiftest runners of the village with an order to deliver them to her "brother" as quickly as they could.

In the days that followed, Pocahontas could not stop thinking about Captain John Smith and Jamestown. Although she played with her friends in the stream, hunted with her brother Nautauquas in the forest, and listened at night to the ancient tribal tales around the fire, her thoughts were of the nearby island. She would finger her silver bracelet and smile to herself.

But thoughts of Jamestown did not just bring joy. Pocahontas remembered how the man who had been knocked over by the barrel had been nearly dead of starvation. She remembered how gaunt and pale everyone had looked. She knew about starvation —but only from tales about allied tribes whose harvests had been sparse or whose hunters had been lazy. Here, at Werowocomoco, there was so much food that even the dogs ate their fill. It made Pocahontas sad to know that there were people not far from her village who were dying of hunger while she had so much.

Finally, after a week of pondering and worrying, Pocahontas asked Powhatan if she might again visit Jamestown, to take more provisions to the famished colony.

Powhatan made no objection. "So be it," he nodded. "We shall feed your 'captives' until their great ship arrives. But remember, Pocahontas, to keep your wits about you. Learn what you can about the white man's magic. There are times when the cunning of the fox is worth more than the claws of the bear."

Pocahontas smiled. When it came to cunning and cleverness, she did not believe that the white strangers matched her father— not even John Smith. But she agreed to find out what she could; her natural curiosity would have led her to do so anyway.

Soon a routine was established, and every three or four days, Pocahontas and her friends would take baskets of food to Jamestown. Sometimes they would go at night, giggling as they set the baskets down by the front gate of the fort before running back into the forest. Sometimes they would walk through Jamestown's single street, smiling and greeting its inhabitants.

The colonists were, in turn, delighted to see Pocahontas, not only for the life-saving food she brought but also because of her enthusiasm for life. She came to symbolize for them the hope they had placed in life in the New World—a hope they had all but lost.

The colonists taught Pocahontas a few words in English, including, "hello," "food," and, for Smith, "the Captain." She, in turn, taught her new friends the Powhatan words for corn, trees, and wind.

The colonists marveled at the beauty of nature that surrounded them: the majestic sunsets, the lush forests, and the awe-inspiring force of a thunderstorm. And for Pocahontas Jamestown was a place of enchantment—from the colonists' fire-breathing guns to their stout brick houses, from the starched collars of their clothing to the way they communicated without speaking by scribbling on scraps of paper.

But life was not to remain idyllic, and the two cultures, so vastly different, were bound to clash—especially when the goal of one was ultimately to claim and conquer the age-old homeland of the other.

It happened, finally, when the long-awaited ship, commanded by Captain Newport, arrived from across the ocean laden with the desperately needed supplies. As it turned out, there were barely enough foodstuffs to go around. During the voyage Captain Newport and his men had made the decision to stay in Jamestown for a while. They were possessed by gold fever and felt sure they would find vast riches in the streams and mountains of the New World. Soon the lust for wealth infected the colonists as well, so instead of preparing the land for planting, they attempted to sift the soil for gold dust. Supplies steadily dwindled and then a fire devastated the town, destroying the one grain crop the colonists had managed to store away for the winter months.

Although he was greatly discouraged by this turn of events, Captain John Smith toiled ceaselessly in an effort to rebuild Jamestown. His greatest task, however, was to try and talk his men into doing the work that must be done to save the colony and to chase the dream of gold from their heads. And with all that, starvation continued to threaten the settlement and Smith had to ask Pocahontas once again to supply them with baskets of food.

Pocahontas gladly took the colonists meats, vegetables, and berries; she would have done anything for her "big brother." But President Wingfield was jealous of Smith's relationship with the Indians. So for every trinket Smith gave Pocahontas and her friends in return for a basket of food, Wingfield would give two—hoping to bribe the Indians and win their trust.

But trinkets are, after all, just that, and Powhatan, a wise and clever ruler, soon found the exchange unequal. What he wanted were the firearms Smith had promised to teach them to use. He wanted swords and guns and ammunition. These were the tools to barter with; these were the stuff of life and death—the same as food. These weapons would vanquish his enemies.

To achieve this end, Powhatan decided to bribe the palefaces in return—by taking twenty fat turkeys to the fort. As payment he wanted twenty metal swords. Captain Newport's instructions from England were not to offend the Indians in any way, and the sight of the turkeys made the half-starved colonists willing to accede to Powhatan's demand. They agreed on the spot.

Two days later, Powhatan's men returned with twenty more turkeys, for which they demanded twenty more swords. Powhatan had begun to understand the true meaning of barter as the colonists practiced it, and he had told his men to be prepared to use any means necessary to get the coveted swords.

This time, the Indians went directly to Smith—who was equally clever and wise. He feared that the Indians might one day turn on the colonists. If they had weapons, they could destroy the settlement. He said no.

The Indians were furious and later that same night they attempted to steal the swords from the fort's armory. But Smith had suspected something might happen when they reacted so strongly to his refusal so he had placed extra guards around the cabin. The Indians were caught and placed in a makeshift jail. They were so frightened by what had befallen them that they easily confessed: Powhatan had given them orders to steal the swords if necessary.

The hostilities had begun.

Although Powhatan was still somewhat fearful of the white man's magic, he knew he had to do something to win back the colonists' faith and trust. And he knew just what to do. He sent his daughter Pocahontas to Jamestown as an ambassador of peace.

On this occasion Pocahontas entered the fort with much more formality. Many braves accompanied her, bearing gifts of food, corn seed for spring planting, and deerskins and bearskins. The princess ordered the braves to place their bundles on the ground. Then she bowed to Captain Smith, looked up, and smiled at the group of colonists who had gathered around.

"These gifts I bear are from the great Powhatan," she said, while Smith translated for the group. "He apologizes for any wrong done by his braves. He is sorry for any misunderstanding."

She spoke so frankly and courageously that Smith would have freed the men even if they had committed far worse a crime. "Do you desire these men freed, Pocahontas?" he asked.

"Oh, yes, my brother!" she replied eagerly. "My heart has always ached for those held captive."

Smith now pretended to grow grave. "But, little sister, we have a problem," he said, attempting to hide a smile. "I must deliver these men to a jailer, someone at Werowocomoco who will treat them as harshly as I once was treated."

Pocahontas looked puzzled. She did not know if Smith was joking or if he was serious.

Finally, Smith allowed himself a small smile. "Will you be their jailer, Pocahontas?"

Pocahontas finally understood and laughed out loud. She took the braves back to Chief Powhatan, who was so pleased with his daughter's diplomacy that he ordered a soft white deerskin skirt and tunic to be made for her.

In September of 1608, John Smith was finally elected president of the Jamestown colony. Now he could do officially what he had been doing all the time on his own, and with much more efficiency. He ordered the building of new houses and the construction of a whitewashed church. He trained the colonists in military exercises. He led explorations into the uncharted Chesapeake Bay. He prepared the fort for the arrival of new colonists—men, women, and families, who would be coming to build a new life in the New World.

But the Indians remained very much in the colonists' thoughts —and in the minds of the English rulers. King James and his board of governors thought that Indians could be drawn closer to English ways if their chiefs were crowned, in coronation ceremonies similar to those at Westminister Abbey in London. They decided that Powhatan, as chief of all the Algonquin tribes, should be the first to be made a king, and they sent a jewel encrusted crown, a red velvet robe, and a lavish scepter in the hold of the next supply ship.

Smith, who knew Powhatan better than any other colonist, was deeply opposed to the plan. He respected Powhatan and knew him to be a wise and dignified man. He knew that a crown instead of a feather headdress would make no difference to the chief, whose power among his own people was such that he needed no external trappings in order to command their respect.

But an order from England carried great weight, so Smith

traveled to Werowocomoco with a small group of men with the express purpose of taking Powhatan back to Jamestown for his English coronation.

But when the colonists entered the village, they found it empty. No braves, no wives, no children, no Powhatan—and no Pocahontas. Smith was sure that the members of the tribe were watching from hiding places in the woods and in their lodgings and it made him uneasy. This was unusual behavior. He did not understand it. He was disappointed as well, for he had been looking forward to visiting with Pocahontas, whom he had not seen for a long time. He wanted to talk with her in her native tongue, without the constant interruptions that were forced on them in Jamestown.

Suddenly, a group of Indians emerged from the woods to welcome the white settlers. They pointed to a small meadow at the edge of the trees which was, Smith knew, often used for special ceremonies. He beckoned his men follow him.

They were frightened, and suspicious of an attack. Smith tried to assuage their fears: these Indians were his friends, nothing would happen. "Hold your head high, with dignity, and follow me," he told them.

But one of the men protested. "It does not seem wise, Captain, to venture so far from our ship. If they mean to harm us, we will have a harder time fighting them off."

"There will be no fighting," Smith said firmly.

But at that moment loud shrieks erupted from the woods and from between the trees twenty Indians in masks, headdresses, and bright paint dashed out and swooped around them.

CHAPTER 13

POWHATAN'S CORONATION

The trees were so close together that it was difficult to separate from the shadows the figures that ran into the clearing. Here whirled a red-painted arm, there danced a glowing mask, topped by antlers. Here moved a blue-painted arm, a tattooed chest, a feathered ankle. All around was a great mass of color and sound, a vivid symphony of movement.

"Indians," shouted one of the men, "with full war paint on!"

"They're going to kill us!" shouted another.

"It's a trap!"

"Shoot them!"

In that instant John Smith's faith in the friendship Powhatan had offered him vanished, and he drew his weapon, ready to fight. "Men!" he shouted and then looked again. Then he halted in midsentence and lifted his hand. "Halt!" he shouted. "Hold your weapons!" In the split second before their fates would have been

changed forever, Smith had recognized the leader of the Indians
—Pocahontas.

There she was, spinning and dancing into the clearing. She
wore large branching antlers on her head, an otter-skin skirt and
shawl, and bows and arrows across her shoulders. Her body was
shiny with bear grease; her skin was painted in swirls and patterns
of blue, red, and white. As she looked at John Smith with his
weapon aimed, Pocahontas nearly stumbled.

"My brother!" she cried, in a tone full of hurt and disappointment. "Did you think we were going to harm you? Did you doubt
me, as well?"

For the first time in his life, John Smith could not find the
words to reply. He cast his eyes down, embarrassed, and dropped
his weapon to the ground. He ordered his men to do the same.

"Forgive us, Pocahontas," he cried. "We were taken by
surprise."

Pocahontas paused, mulling over Smith's explanation. Then
she nodded. "I understand, my brother. I suppose that I, too,
would be afraid if a hundred palefaces bearing guns and screaming war cries came toward me!" She smiled. "And as soon as you
saw it was me, you told your men to cease their fire." She murmured quietly, "You do trust me, after all."

Smith bowed. "Always, Pocahontas."

They looked at each other for a brief moment. Then, just as
fast as she had grown serious, Pocahontas once more became a
wood sprite. "Let the harvest ritual begin anew!"

Her comrades began to laugh and shout and dance. The drums
played on, and Smith and his men beheld the spectacle of a
hundred Indians performing the same ancient dance, as old as
time, that their fathers and their forefathers had before them—a
dance as timeless as the harvests that came year after year, bountiful and blessed.

Like their leader, Pocahontas, the dancers all wore antlers. Their arms, legs, and torsos were also painted bright blue, white, and red. They danced around a roaring fire in the center of the clearing, singing a song so beautiful and joyous that the white men were hypnotized by its sound.

Smith recognized some of the words—phrases of welcome, songs of birth and renewal, praises to the fertile earth and fast-growing seed. But some of the music was beyond his understanding and he sat as spellbound as his companions, knowing that they were privileged to witness something so mystical, primal, and rare.

Although it seemed an eternity to the awestruck colonists, the ritual lasted but an hour. And, as quickly as they had come into the clearing, the Indians left, fading into the darkness of the forest.

Suddenly, in the dim light of dusk, the colonists saw that they were not alone. Braves, women, children, and elders also had been sitting around the fire, watching the harvest dance. The firelight flickered over their faces. One of the braves rose from his position by the fire, and approached Smith and his men. It was Pocahontas's brother, Nautauquas.

He greeted them with a friendly bow and bid them follow him to his father's lodge. "Now that the ritual is done, the harvest is secure. All is well and my father can now see you. Please."

The men readily stood and accompanied Nautauquas to Powhatan's lodge. Smith immediately recognized the lodge as the one where his life had been in jeopardy not very long before. He entered the dark, smoky wigwam with trepidation, his heart beating hard.

As Powhatan began to speak, Smith's fear abated. "Tell your comrades they are welcome," Powhatan said in his native tongue. "And you, my son, are always welcome. You are one of our own."

He gestured to the Englishmen to sit on the mats that had been cleaned and spread for their arrival. Baskets of food were brought in and the feasting began.

The dishes were elaborate and tasty: twenty-four hour baked beans; a traditional succotash, made of corn, beans, and sweet green and red peppers; sweet maple sugar; fried cornbread; succulent turkey; bright cranberries; and even freshly baked clams. The Englishmen ate with relish, and when the last morsel had been swallowed, one of Smith's men turned to him.

"Has Powhatan asked why we are here? About the honor we want to give him?" The man snickered behind his hand; he knew the coronation was only a hollow goodwill gesture, that the English intended to reign supreme in this land.

Smith frowned at him. "It is not polite for an Indian to ask a guest such questions. But now that we have eaten, I will happily tell him of the honor we plan for him. And," he looked sternly at each man, "it is indeed an honor to be crowned as king, one that need not be taken lightly—even if it is being held in this New World instead of in Westminster Abbey!"

With that much said, Smith got up abruptly and bowed to Powhatan with much dignity. Pocahontas, who had stood at the entrance to the lodge looking on as the men feasted, now entered and sat by her father. She had removed her elaborate antler headdress.

"Ruler of many tribes," Smith began, "great Chief Powhatan, we have come with greetings sent you from across the sea by our own great chieftain, King James. In our world beyond the sea, the greatest chief who rules many tribes is called a king. He is mightier than all other rulers and he has many riches and much honor. When our king dies, a new one takes his place in a ceremony called a coronation. A jeweled, golden circlet called a crown is placed on his head. He is given a precious staff of honor to hold.

And on his shoulders he wears royal robes of velvet and satin and fur, so that all who see him shall know that this is the king and all must revere and obey him."

Smith paused for a moment, glancing around the room at each Indian before resting his attention once again on Chief Powhatan. "Our own King James," he continued, "has heard much of you and the many tribes you rule. He very much wishes that you, too, should be crowned king. This will symbolize to all that you are his equal and friend. The English will know you are his brother and your own people will hold you in even greater awe."

Powhatan showed no interest at all in these words. But from the eager look on Pocahontas's face, Smith knew that his speech had at least been understood.

Ignoring the chief's seeming lack of enthusiasm, Smith continued. "Therefore, we plan to hold your coronation at Jamestown on a day that is agreeable to you. Our king has sent gifts for you which await you in Jamestown."

At long last Smith had no more words. He glanced expectantly at Chief Powhatan, waiting for an answer. The chief thought for a moment in silence, then spoke. "If your king has sent me presents, they should come to me here, at Werowocomoco. I, too, am a king and this is my land. I am honored by your ruler's good wishes, but the coronation must take place here, on my land."

Powhatan spoke with such quiet dignity that Smith did not try to dissuade him. Instead, he found himself respecting the chieftain even more for his diplomatic skill. Going to Jamestown would have been a subservient gesture. By insisting that the coronation be on his own land, in his village, he was proving that he was truly equal to King James—and a worthy ruler of his people.

Smith bowed to the chief and agreed to do as he wished. He and his men thanked him for his hospitality and thanked Pocahontas for allowing them the privilege of seeing the harvest dance. Then they departed for Jamestown, planning to return in a few days' time with what they needed to perform the coronation ceremony.

Pocahontas eagerly awaited their return. In fact, she could think and speak about nothing else. "Perhaps," she said to Nautauquas and Claw-of-the-Eagle one day while they were out hunting, "there is some strange medicine in this ceremony that will make our father immortal and safe from even death itself."

"I have more faith in the white men's guns than in their medicine," declared Claw-of-the-Eagle. "Ever since one of them let me try to fire one, I have understood that they are not worked by magic. They are a clever tool made by men. If we could only manage to get enough of them, we would be many times stronger than the palefaces—and we could destroy all of them before another shipload of newcomers arrived."

"No," cried Pocahontas, "not as long as your brother, John Smith, lives. Even you said that you could not look at his eyes."

Pocahontas had hit her mark. Claw-of-the-Eagle had never been able to look Smith in the eye since the day he had crawled away from the lodge without killing him. Smith was the only man who awed him so, and he dreamed of the day when he might be able to deal him a blow in the dark and those powerful eyes would not stop him. But he felt equal to any other paleface—in the darkness or the light.

Slowly, gravely, Nautauquas joined in the conversation. "But why should we wish to destroy these white men?" he asked thoughtfully. "It is true I had different thoughts once and I went alone into the forest to fast and pray so that I might find the answer to the question, 'Are they friend or foe?' " Nautauquas sighed. "But all I know is that somehow the white tribes that live across the great waters have found their way here. They have come to the north and to the south and they continue to come."

Nautauquas paused and looked out at the forest, as if he could see the blue waters beyond the trees. "I have heard that the white tribes who come to the south are cruel. They have destroyed many villages and have killed our people. My father has said to me that we cannot hide our trail from these wanderers. And, since they continue to come, it is better to be their friends than their enemies. We must be allies so they will leave us in peace and not do to us what those in the south have done."

In spite of himself, Claw-of-the-Eagle was impressed with this reasoning. "Do you then like these paleface strangers and their ways?" he asked.

"There is much about them I do not understand," replied Nautauquas. "How can they wear so many garments? Why do they build houses that let in no air? Why do they come here when they have villages beyond the sea? I do not know the answers, but I do believe they are worthy of our respect." Nautauquas paused, rubbing his arms as if a chill breeze had just blown past. "And, in truth, we have no choice."

It was some days later that John Smith, Captain Newport, and fifty other men started out for Werowocomoco for the coronation of Powhatan. Smith had great misgivings about the journey; he felt the idea of a coronation was bald exploitation. And he feared it would make Powhatan feel even more powerful.

But Captain Newport wanted the coronation to be performed exactly as King James had instructed. He felt it would bring the two cultures closer together and make the Indians friendlier to them. He refused to listen to any of Smith's arguments.

So the group began the long and arduous journey through the forest, made even more cumbersome by the traditional formal garb worn by the English—stiff black breeches; starched and slashed puffed sleeves; huge, white ruffled collars; and clumsy high-heeled boots. Theirs swords and heavy silver buckles and buttons glistened in the sun.

The gifts sent by the King of England were so heavy that they had to be sent separately upriver by boat. Among them were a real wooden bed and chest of drawers, a china basin and a delicate pitcher, and more.

Holding up the rear of the entire procession was a group of soldiers weighed down with muskets and heavy axes, on the alert for any danger.

As the company approached Werowocomoco, the Indians emerged from their lodges. They, too, had bedecked themselves in their finest clothing for the mysterious coronation. Braves, women, and children alike wore colorful necklaces and beads. They had covered their bodies in bright paint and had spread elaborately embroidered robes over their shoulders.

It presented a wonderful picture as the two groups came together—the soberly dressed, but now dusty Englishmen marching through a crowd of curious, colorfully garbed Indians, whose children peeked out from behind their mother's skirts, staring at the strange clothes and the solemn faces. And there, also, was Pocahontas, running through the crowd, to and fro, from front to back, dressed in her finest suede moccasins and white-beaded robe, not wanting to miss a thing.

As Powhatan and Captain Newport greeted each other, each man eyed the other shrewdly. The gifts were unloaded from the boat and spread out at Powhatan's feet. Pocahontas knew many of the Englishmen from her visits to Jamestown and she went from person to person, smiling, shaking hands hello, as if she were the object of all the ceremony.

Some of the elders scowled at her. They did not like the friendliness she showed the palefaced strangers. But Powhatan, always the indulgent father, did not restrain her. Finally, after a few words with Smith, she rejoined Cleopatra and her other sisters.

And then the questions began to fly. The tribe knew that she had more knowledge than they of English ways and habits. When the wrappings were removed from the bed, Cleopatra and the others gasped and shouted as one, "What is that thing, Pocahontas? What is it?"

Pocahontas smiled. She was pleased with her new role. "That, my sisters, is a couch on which they sleep."

"Is it more comfortable than our mats?" asked Cleopatra. "I would be afraid that I would fall off it into the fire while I slept!"

Pocahontas agreed. She had never tried a bed and she thought as her sister did. It looked dangerous indeed. But the pitcher and basin fascinated her. They were so beautiful and delicate that the Indians exclaimed over them and each woman wanted them for her own.

Then came the time for the official event. Captain Newport unwrapped the package containing a soft red velvet robe. With John Smith as translator, he explained that King James had worn a similar robe when he was made king of all England.

Powhatan smiled with pleasure. He took off his fur mantle and allowed the Englishmen to put the new robe on his shoulders. Captain Newport held up a mirror so that he could see for himself how grand he looked.

The trumpets sounded and an English drummer beat a loud tattoo. Smith and Newport approached the tall chieftain. Newport held a jeweled copper crown in his outstretched hands.

"Kneel, mighty Powhatan," proclaimed Captain Smith, "so that we may crown you king."

Suddenly, the mood changed. Powhatan, who had been touching the soft velvet of his new robe, stood straighter. His smile became an angry glare and he raised his fist. "I am the leader of thirty tribes and lord of sixty villages," he thundered. "I do not kneel for anyone. If you believe me equal to your chieftain, then I will stand."

Smith took off his wide-brimmed hat and wiped the sweat from his brow. He bowed to Powhatan and said, "We mean you no disrespect, Powhatan. Even the King of England kneeled at his coronation. It is the way."

Powhatan shook his head. "No," he said firmly. He crossed his arms in front of his chest and stared at the Englishmen. His warriors became more watchful. They were ready for his command.

Smith bit his lip. Without thinking, he put his hand on Powhatan's shoulder. Newport did the same on his opposite shoulder. Powhatan was forced to bend the slightest bit and, at that moment of supplication, Newport quickly placed the copper crown on his head. "I now pronounce you king and ruler of all your land," he said.

The soldiers shot off their muskets. The rest of the company pulled off their hats and cheered.

Although startled by the noise of the guns, Powhatan and his men quickly composed themselves. Wearing his rich red robe and his heavy copper crown, Powhatan seated himself on a mat that a tribesman had laid out for him. His back was straight and tall. His chin jutted proudly and he looked very much the king that he was.

Powhatan looked so dignified that Smith was compelled to whisper to his companion, "My dear God. If he is not more kingly looking than our royal James himself!" He began to think that the coronation had not been a bad idea at all.

The feast was then brought and, once again, the Englishmen did full justice to the Indian dishes. Pocahontas, carrying her bowl of food, came and sat down beside Smith.

"Welcome, little sister," he said. "How do you like your father's new robe?"

"In truth, he appears strange to me," she answered. "But he will not wear it for long. It is beautiful, that cloak, but he can paint his skin just as fine a color and it will not be as warm or as heavy."

Smith laughed. "Do you think you would want to wear clothes such as those our women wear—long skirts, buttoned shoes, and delicate lace? You will surely see them because they will be coming on a ship to Jamestown soon."

"Do white men have wives, too?" asked Pocahontas in astonishment.

"Of course! We have families just as you do."

"And you, my brother," she queried eagerly, "will your family come soon?"

"I do not have any family, Matoaka," Smith said sadly, using Pocahontas's special name. "My life has led me to so many places and through so many dangers that I never seemed to have the time to meet someone and marry."

"That is so sad, my brother," Pocahontas said, shaking her head. "A wife could help you see your dangers through. She could make sure that you had fresh fish, sweet walnut milk, and dried venison on your return, a warm fire, and clean leggings for your body. She would make sure that your mats were comfortable. That would help you on your journeys—not hinder you!" she said passionately.

Captain Smith smiled ruefully. He remembered the nightlong talk they had had so long ago, when she had been his jailer and he her prisoner. "You paint a wonderful picture, Matoaka. And it is true," he said. "Sometimes I feel very lonely in my wigwam and, when the stars are clouded and the night is long, I very much want a wife."

Pocahontas gazed at him. "None would ever refuse you," she whispered.

Smith blinked, and for a brief moment he thought of how it would be to throw his lot in with this new country, to learn to live among the trees and stars, to join in ceremonies and become one with his proud, simple friends. But even as he entertained the thought of running free through the forest, he also realized that Pocahontas was still a young girl—she was still a child—and their cultures would inevitably clash. He sighed and touched her cheek. "You are a very special child, Matoaka. Do not forget that, ever."

The mood was shattered by Captain Newport, bellowing orders to the company that it was now time to take their leave. The men groaned as they got up from their comfortable mats. They had eaten and drunk a great deal and their bodies were stiff from sitting during the ceremony. Smith rose, too, bidding farewell to Pocahontas.

During the feasting, Powhatan had been thinking about how he might reciprocate the honor he had received. As the white men gathered up their belongings, Powhatan stood, too. Gravely, the chief presented to Captain Newport a bundle of wheat ears for spring planting. Then, with the utmost dignity, he handed him his old moccasins and the fur mantle he had laid aside when they had placed the coronation robe upon his shoulders. Newport was amazed; he did not know what he was to do with them. But the diplomatic Smith made a speech of gratitude and thanks. "It is an honor to receive these kingly garments," he said gravely. "Let it always be a symbol of peace between white man and Indian and let us always live together in harmony."

CHAPTER 14

A Dangerous Supper

Some months passed. It was now January 1609 and, as in previous winters, the Jamestown larder was empty. Starvation was once again threatening the colony and people would die if help were not found. John Smith thought of the full storehouses at Werowocomoco and decided it was time to pay Powhatan another visit to purchase some supplies.

So, on a frigid morning, with the snow just starting to fall, Smith set out on a boat with twelve men to go upriver to the Indian village.

The river was treacherous; as they came closer to the village, they encountered more and more ice; great sheets stretched for half a mile or more toward the shore. But so desperate was the plight of the colonists that Smith refused to turn back. He would not return to Jamestown without a good supply of corn and other food. He would steal what he wanted, if it proved necessary, or even take it at gunpoint.

Smith had not seen Chief Powhatan for some time. There were rumors from the scouts who traveled the back forests that of late Powhatan was not pleased with the English.

The Dutch had arrived in the area, and they had not been idle. While the Spaniards and the French had invaded the southern coasts of the New World, the Dutch had been hired by King James to further explore the settlement possibilities of the north and central regions. They had pushed through the forest near Jamestown and, ignoring their pact with the English, had befriended Powhatan and his tribe on their own.

In fact, to remain in his good graces, they actually had built Powhatan a small wooden house. And while they hammered in nails and smoothed the wood, they betrayed their English benefactors. They talked and they talked, filling Powhatan's head with ugly rumors and tales about the British. It was a story as old as time: the desire of one power to best another. If the British were destroyed by the Indians, then the Dutch would reign supreme. They would have the tobacco and the food, the land and its bounty.

Thus they told Powhatan and the other elders not to trust the British, they told them that Smith, en route to Werowocomoco, was preparing to do battle, to seize the provisions he wanted by force.

Pocahontas saw her father and the Dutchmen conferring together. She saw them huddled and whispering, and she heard the word "Smith" over and over. She saw her father nod. It made her worry for her brother, John Smith. She did not know what would happen and she waited anxiously for the boat from Jamestown to appear.

Finally, the news was shouted throughout the village that the boat carrying Smith and his companions was slowly approaching through the broken ice.

Pocahontas hurried eagerly to the river and waved to her friends. She watched them come ashore but stopped herself from running to meet them. She had a sense that this was not the moment for kind words and warm hugs. She was afraid that Powhatan's enmity toward the English had been fanned by the Dutchmen until it was ready to explode. She decided the best policy was to appear indifferent to the palefaces—and to let her own people think that she, too, had grown hostile to them. But she would also stay close to her father so as to learn what he intended to do.

Powhatan approached the colonists dressed, not in his red mantle or English crown, but instead in a traditional headdress of eagle feathers, leggings, and a cape of brown bear fur. His face betrayed no emotion as he strode slowly to the bank of the river and called out a greeting to John Smith.

"You are welcome to Werowocomoco, my son, but why do you come with guns when you visit your father?"

John Smith and his company were not fools. They understood at once the significance of Powhatan's dress and felt the hostility that showed itself in Powhatan's bearing and in the silence of his tribesmen. Thus they came ashore with their guns, not ready to fire, but held, at least, as a sign that they were ready to defend themselves if need be. Ignoring the chieftain's question, Smith declared, "We have come to buy food from you, Chief Powhatan, in exchange for precious beads and knives and cloths of many colors."

Powhatan interrupted his speech. "But first, lay aside your arms," he demanded. "What need have you of guns if you have come with such a peaceful purpose? Are you thinking of frightening my people into selling you their food?" He spread his arms out from under the fullness of his fur robe. "Why take by force what you can have just as quickly through friendship? Every year our friendly people have supplied you with corn, and yet this time, you carry your guns and swords as if to invade an enemy."

When Smith had translated Chief Powhatan's words, many in his company were ashamed by their show of force. They would have been willing to leave them aboard ship while they were on this friendly chieftain's land. But Smith was not so sure. He was now learning how to read the Indians' subtle signs and, although he did not know why, he knew that the chief had reasons for wanting them unarmed. He pulled off his hat, wiped his brow in thought, and called out in answer, "When your people come to Jamestown, all of them carry their bows and arrows. So we though it proper to wear our arms as part of our apparel as you do. We mean our arms as a sign of respect."

There followed more words between the two and much talk about "father" and "son," but Pocahontas, who heard it all, did not feel reassured. She had loved Smith as a brother since the day she had saved his life—and she was sure that her father now planned to harm him. Her brother Nautauquas was away with Claw-of-the-Eagle, fighting the Massawomekes, an enemy tribe. Had he been at Werowocomoco, she might have confided her fear and confusion to him. But, as it was, she realized that she, and she alone, must discover her father's intentions—and do something about them.

She saw that Powhatan had left the group, and that Smith and his men were now standing at the entrance to the lodge which Powhatan had assigned to them. They were carrying from the boat to the lodge the objects they had brought for bartering.

Suddenly, several Indian braves rushed towards Smith, arrows notched in their bowstrings. One let his arrow fly; it was aimed too high and hit only the bark of the lodge wall above Smith's head. Before another arrow could leave its bow, Smith whipped out his pistol and pointed it at the advancing crowd. His men rushed from the lodge, their muskets raised.

Seeing that the Englishmen were still armed, the Indians turned and fled, disappearing into the forest. Pocahontas, trembling with anger, ran through the trees to find her father and ask him the meaning of this treacherous treatment of his guests.

When she had gone a little distance, she caught sight of Chief Powhatan. She hid behind a rock, waiting to see where he was going. To her amazement, she saw that he was turning to the white men's lodge and that behind him followed several Indians carrying great baskets of food and corn seed. What could he mean, she wondered, by first trying to kill, then to feast, the white men? She followed, unseen, as Powhatan approached Smith without the slightest hesitation or appearance of guilt.

"It rejoices my heart, my son," she heard him call out when he was within one hundred feet of Smith, "to know that you are unharmed. While I was gone to see that your provisions were properly handled, my young braves, crazed with religious zeal, and fasting in preparation for a great ceremony, knew not what they were doing, and so shot at you." Powhatan put his hand out to Smith; he gestured towards the Indians behind him. "Please, my son, think no evil of us. Why would we seek to harm you one moment, then help you the next? Behold the supplies that I, your father, have brought for you, and accept my apologies."

And Smith, although he was still puzzled and mistrustful of this recent behavior, nodded. "I accept your apology, Chief Powhatan, as no harm was done." But Pocahontas, still hiding behind her rock, knew that no one in Werowocomoco would have dared shoot at the white men except by direct order of Chief Powhatan —and still she did not understand what was happening.

However, perhaps all was now well. Maybe her father had at least realized that the Englishmen could be formidable enemies and perhaps they had formed an unspoken truce. She watched Powhatan and Smith supervising the placing of great stores of food into the boat and the filling of the now empty baskets with cloth, beads, top hats, boots, and other European goods.

Finally, their work was finished and Pocahontas saw a brave run from the woods and drop exhausted before Chief Powhatan, gasping out a few words. Although the messenger did not have breath enough to cry them out, his words were heard by the Indians standing nearby and they shouted them aloud to everyone. Immediately, the crowd rose to its feet and began to utter loud shrieks, dancing up and down in circles, as others began to shake rattles and beat upon drums.

"What is the meaning of all this, Smith?" asked one of his men, who stood with the others, watching the strange performance.

"Tell them, my son," said Powhatan, understanding from the tone of the Englishman's voice that his words were a question, "that twenty of my braves, among them Nautauquas and Claw-of-the-Eagle, have won a great victory over one hundred of our enemies, and that this is our song of triumph."

The old chief's eyes shone more brightly than ever, and his back was as firm and straight as that of one of his sons.

"I shall soon have witnessed all their different dances," John Smith confided to his men, after repeating Powhatan's words. "There lacks now only the war dance."

There was a pause in the dancing and then Powhatan gave a signal and the drums and rattles started up once more. The rhythm, this time, was different; even the white men could tell this, and they noticed that the Indians moved more swiftly, as if animated by the greatest excitement. Fresh dancers, their faces and bodies painted red and black, took the places of those who fell from fatigue, and the woods resounded with their loud song.

"It must have been a great victory," said Smith, "to have so excited them."

But Pocahontas knew the truth and her heart beat as if it were a war drum itself, for she knew what the white men did not know: that this last dance *was* a war dance.

At last the dancing ceased and a meal was passed around. All was now so peaceful that the Englishmen laid aside their weapons, setting only one guard to watch while the rest of them sat around the great fire they had built in the lodge. They waited calmly for the next morning's high tide to lift their boat out of the half-frozen ooze in which low tide had trapped it. Powhatan and his tribesmen had left, but he had sent a messenger with a necklace and bracelet of freshwater pearls and words of affection for his "son." He said he would shortly send them some more food from his own pots, so that they would lack for nothing that night.

The darkness came quickly and the woods that stretched between the lodge and the center of Werowocomoco were thick and black. It was through them that Pocahontas sped more swiftly than she had ever run in her life. She did not trip over roots slippery with frost, nor did she feel the cold on her bare shoulders. For she had overheard her father speaking to his braves and knew, without a doubt, that the war dance had been danced against the English. An attack was being planned.

She was breathless when she reached the lodge near the river's edge. Rushing inside, she seized a musket from the pile on the ground and, to the astonishment of the guard, thrust it into Smith's hands, crying, "Arm yourselves, my friends. Make ready fast."

Smith began to question her, but she held up her hand and panted, "When your weapons are ready, I will speak."

Smith hurriedly gave orders, silently reproaching himself for his false confidence. The men sprang up from the fire, seized their long-barreled muskets and threw belts of bullets over their shoulders. The merry, careless party had quickly become a troop of cautious soldiers. Then Smith turned to Pocahontas.

No longer breathless, she answered his unspoken question. "I have long overheard the words of the treacherous Dutchmen to my father. And when I heard the war song and saw them dancing the war dance, I grew fearful. Woe is me, my brother, that I should speak against my own father, but I have heard him make plans to take you by surprise without your weapons." She pulled back her damp hair from her brow, then continued. "He has waited all day for this attack. He had hoped to ensnare you with kind words. The braves are on their way now with the extra food the chief promised you. He has given orders to his men that while you are eating they should fall upon you and slay you all—and none may escape. As soon as I learned this, I hastened here to warn you." Pocahontas breathed deeply; she bit her lip. She had said all she needed to say.

Smith was deeply touched by the girl's loyalty. He knew the anger she would face if Powhatan ever learned what she had done.

"Matoaka," he cried, clasping her hand. "You have this night put all England in your debt. As long as Jamestown is a name people remember, so long will they recall how you saved it from destruction." He kissed her hand. "In truth, your father had lulled my suspicions, and if you had not come to warn us, we would surely have perished." He gazed into her eyes. "We all thank you, Princess, and, to my little sister, I give my own deep gratitude once again."

Smith pulled a thick gold chain that he had bought in Turkey from around his collar and placed it around Pocahontas's bare neck. "Take this chain in remembrance," he said. Then his comrades approached Pocahontas, each one with a gift he placed in the maiden's hands.

Pocahontas gazed at them all with love. She shook her head slowly, crying silently. "I dare not, my friends," she said. "If my father found these gifts he would kill me because he would know that it was I who brought you warning."

Slowly, she removed the chain and reluctantly returned it to Smith. She let the other treasures she longed to keep fall gently to the ground. Smith bent and kissed her hand again, as reverently as he had once kissed that of the good Queen Elizabeth.

Pocahontas started. "I hear them coming!" she cried, and with one swift movement she disappeared again into the night. She skirted the river until she was sure of reaching her lodge without meeting the troop of Indians advancing with dishes and baskets of food.

When they reached the white men's lodge, the braves brought in the supper and laid it down with great heartiness. Some of the braves were halted by Smith at the entrance, where he engaged them in conversation. When they suggested that the white men lay aside their weapons and seat themselves to eat, Smith replied that it was the custom of the English at night to eat while standing, food in one hand and musket in the other. This parleying went on for a long time. Smith would not reveal that he had discovered the Powhatans' nefarious plan.

Soon the baffled Indians retired to the forest, waiting for the moment when they could catch the white men off guard. But even though they stared at the lodge all night, not once did they see the white guards move away from their posts. And they had too much fear of their "demon weapons" to attempt an onslaught against men so well defended.

So, thanks to Pocahontas, the morning dawned on an undiminished number of English, and at high tide, they embarked on their return journey to Jamestown with their provisions, so precariously and courageously won.

CHAPTER 15

A FAREWELL

The late summer sun had been beating down pitilessly on Wer-owocomoco for weeks and by now no one had any energy to do anything more than languish in whatever shade they could find. The old braves smoked tobacco or dozed in their wigwams. The women sat under the trees and chatted, leaving the cooking and the making of cornmeal for later in the day. The children, too, were quiet, using the long green leaves of the ears of corn as fans, plaiting the silky ends, and humming the chant of the Green Corn Festival which had been celebrated some weeks before.

Only the young braves refused to succumb to the heat, too proud to show any that it affected them. They kept themselves busy making arrowheads and ran races in the sun—until a wise elder called out that they were young fools with no more sense than silly birds. Then they, too, admitted they were hot and parched, and they drank their fill of cool water from hollowed-out gourds.

Even the energetic Pocahontas was feeling lazy. Off in the woods, near a little stream where trout and crawfish moved about on the sandy bottom, she lay facedown in the shade, her brown arms stretched out, the carpet of pine needles that covered the ground a pillow for her head. When she opened her eyes from time to time, she saw the blue sky through the leaves of the giant red oak that shaded her. Once she saw an eagle that seemed to be soaring straight to the sun.

Pocahontas had cooled off in the stream and now she lay content and drowsy. Her sleepy feeling dulled her perceptions of the sights and sounds of the woodland. The tapping of a woodpecker on a distant tree, the squalling of a catbird, the soft scurrying of a rabbit or squirrel, the buzzing of a nectar-laden bee—all blended into one harmonious melody of summer. She let her thoughts wander.

She remembered the fateful night when John Smith had first come to Werowocomoco, and then when she had "adopted" him as her own. She remembered before that, when Claw-of-the-Eagle had come to the tribe, and how he had been saved from death by old Wansutis, who afterward had adopted him. She thought about the differences between the two—how Claw-of-the-Eagle had easily became one with his new tribe, and how Smith yearned so much for Jamestown that she had had to let him go.

Pocahontas thought about Jamestown. It had been a long time since she had been there. On her last visit, she had actually met two Englishwomen who had recently arrived by boat, a Miss Forrest and her maid, Anne Burroughs.

How the women stared at each other! Pocahontas could not not stop looking at Mistress Forrest's fine hair—at the way it was curled and shaped with delicate little combs. The clothing, too, was so different—so many layers and laces and bows! She loved the brightness of their skirts: blues, yellows, and purples so unlike the colors worn by her people. Their shoes, too, were a source of amazement: high-buttoned leather with heels and bows that matched their skirts. Pocahontas could not see enough of them!

For their part, Mistress Forrest and Anne Burroughs were equally fascinated by the young, free-spirited Indian girl, by her dense black hair braided into two plaits, by her buckskin leggings, her beaded skirts, and soft-as-butter moccasins. They were envious of her cool, loose-fitting clothes. How comfortable and breezy they seemed compared to their own tight corsets and petticoats!

Pocahontas's mind continued to wander, now to her palefaced "brother," John Smith. She thought about his courage and the way the other colonists heeded his words. He was a leader like her father, a man above other men, wise and strong, meting out justice when it was necessary, but always ready to praise good work, too. She smiled as she thought about Smith, of the gentle words he always had for her, of the way he seemed so interested in everything she had to say. He had talked to her as she knew he talked to few others, about his hopes for Jamestown, and how, if they two, he and his "little sister," could work together, the English and the Powhatan tribe could live beside each other and be friends as long as the sky and the earth should last. He even told her one day that marriages between the English and the Indians could cement this friendship. "Perhaps you, yourself, Matoaka," he had begun, and then suddenly stopped. Now she wondered again, as she had wondered then, if he might have meant himself. . . .

Such a possibility excited her and she would happily have thought about it longer, but her eyelids had grown heavy and the pine needles were soft and fragrant, and soon she closed her eyes and fell asleep. A beaver that had been watching her from beneath the exposed roots of an oak tree by the stream saw that Pocahontas was finally still, and he crawled out, ready to begin anew his work on the dam that her feet had unknowingly flattened.

About an hour later, Nautauquas passed by as he returned from visiting another Algonquin tribe. Although he scarcely made more noise than the industrious beaver, Pocahontas suddenly awoke, raising her head from her pine-needle pillow. She shook some stray needles from her hair and dusted herself off.

"Greetings, Matoaka!" her brother called out. "You were as snugly hidden here as a deer."

"Any news, Brother?" she asked as he sat down and, taking off his moccasins, wet his tired feet in the stream.

He paused and took a deep breath before speaking. "It is evil news I bring," he answered gravely, "for the friends of the great Captain."

"What has happened to my white brother?" Pocahontas cried. "Tell me quickly!"

"He was sleeping in his boat, so I heard, far off from Jamestown," continued Nautauquas. A big bag of the powder they put into their guns lay in the bottom of his canoe, and when by chance a spark from his pipe dropped on it, the bag grew angry and began to spit. It burned his flesh until the pain woke him and he had to spring into the river to quench the blaze.

Pocahontas shivered. "Where is he now?" she asked, grabbing hold of her brother's arm. "I wish to go to him." She began to shake him in her impatience.

Nautauquas hesitated. He had never quite trusted Pocahontas's friendship with Smith. Finally, resigned to the inevitable, he sighed and said, "They say he is on his way to Jamestown and should reach there tomorrow."

The peace of the day had vanished. Pocahontas wanted only to go home. When she and Nautauquas returned to Werowocomoco, Pocahontas stopped at Wansutis's lodge.

"I know why you are here," the old woman said as she drew aside her doorway covering. "You have come to get healing herbs for your white friend."

Pocahontas nodded. She had not said a word.

"I have them all ready for you," Wansutis continued, as she thrust a bundle into the girl's hands. "But," Wansutis warned, "though they will cure any of our people, they will not have power over the white man's pain unless he has faith in them."

Wansutis then dropped the skin over her doorway and stepped back into the gloom of her lodge. But she shouted out one last thing, "I do this not only for you, Pocahontas, but also for the white captain. His magic is powerful and he is a good man. I wish him to live so that he may tell me some of his secrets."

Pocahontas still had not said one word. She walked away in silence.

But she could not wait to begin her journey, and before the night was over, Pocahontas had already started on her way to Jamestown. She went alone, as she was in no mood to chatter with a companion. Thunderstorms had come through and cooled the air and softened the earth. She would have enjoyed her night-time journey if she had not been so worried.

It was still early in the morning when Pocahontas reached Jamestown, now a settlement of fifty sturdy houses. On the wharf she saw men hurrying back and forth from a docked ship. They were carrying up to the deck heavy bundles of bearskins and foxskins which had been purchased from her people, boxes tied with rope, and unwieldy trunks. One of the trunks looked familiar to her, like one she had seen in John Smith's house. It was made of rich Cordova leather and had an ornate iron lock. Doubtless, she thought, he would be sending it back to England, filled with gifts for the king he spoke of with such respect.

Without further delay, Pocahontas hastened toward Smith's

house, but before she reached it, she saw that his bed had been carried outside the door and that he lay on it covered in blankets and cushioned by pillows. She recognized, too, the man who was just leaving him—the town's medicine man, or "doctor" as they called him. In her eagerness to see Smith, Pocahontas ran the rest of the way. Catching sight of her, Smith feebly waved his hand.

"Alas! My brother," she cried as she took his hand in hers and saw how thin it had grown. "My poor, poor brother. I am so sorry you have harmed yourself."

"Ah, my friend and sister, Matoaka. You have heard, then," he answered, smiling bravely in spite of the pain. "And you have come, as you always do, to bring aid and comfort."

"I have herbs for your wound," she replied, taking them from her pouch. "They will quickly heal it. They are powerful medicine." She did not repeat Wantusis's admonition that he had to believe in their power for them to work. She was sure that he believed, and she did not want to insult him by telling him to do so. And Wansutis sometimes spoke in riddles, after all.

"Thank you, little sister," he answered gently, "for your loving thoughts and for the journey you have taken. Before you came, my heart was sad, for I said to myself, 'How can I go without bidding farewell to Matoaka? But how can I send a message that will bring her here in time?'"

"Go!" she exclaimed. "Where are you going!"

"Home. To England," Smith replied, wincing as he pushed himself further up on his pillow. "The doctor decided only this morning that his skill is not great enough to heal my wound. And I must return to London where the more experienced medicine men will heal me."

"No, no," cried Pocahontas. "You must not go. Our wise women and our medicine men have secrets and magic you do not know about. Use these herbs and your wound will soon be as clean as the palm of my hand."

"I only wish it could be so, little sister," said Smith sadly. "And, in truth, I have seen amazing cures among your people. If my fever was the result of an arrow's bite, I would gladly let your herbs do their magic." He paused, grimacing in pain. "But gunpowder is a thing unknown to your people and a medicine man's remedies would be useless."

For a moment, Pocahontas did not speak. She sighed deeply and bent her head. "Then you are going and I cannot stop you?" she asked in a voice filled with despair.

"Yes, Matoaka, I am going—or else must take up residence yonder—" and he weakly pointed to the graveyard. "It is a bitter thing to go now and leave my work unfinished."

"I shall die when you are gone!" cried Pocahontas, kneeling down beside his bed and taking his hand. "You have become like a god to me, a god strong and wonderful."

"Little sister! Little sister!" Smith repeated as he stroked her hair. Once again there came to him the thought he had had before—that someday when this child was grown, they would marry. Now this would never come to pass . . .

Pocahontas continued to kneel by his side in silence. Then her face brightened and she asked with hope and eagerness in her voice, "Will you come back to us when you are well?"

"I promise you, Matoaka, that if I live, we shall see each other again. This I promise."

He did not say to her what was in his mind, that no English maiden, no matter how golden-haired or rosy-cheeked, would ever be as dear to him as she.

On hearing her "brother's" promise, Pocahontas's spirits rose. She tried not to think about the weeks and months that would pass before she would see him again. Instead, she seated herself beside him on the ground and listened while he talked to her of his love and concern for the Jamestown colony.

"Do you see, Matoaka," said Smith, his voice growing stronger with enthusiasm, "that this town is like my child? It is that dear to me. I have spent sleepless nights and weary days caring for it. I have suffered cold and hunger and the enmity of jealous men for it. And I have come close to death for it."

Smith took Pocahontas's hand and gazed intently into her eyes. "And you, too, have cared for Jamestown, until it has become partly your own, and very dear to you. Now that I must depart, I leave Jamestown to your care. Will you continue to watch over it, to do all within your power for its welfare?"

Pocahontas took both of Smith's hands firmly in her own. "That I will gladly do, my brother. That is my promise to you. Not a day shall pass that I will not walk through the forest to see that all is well. My ears shall listen every night for approaching harm. 'Jamestown is Pocahontas's friend,' I shall whisper to the north wind, and it will not blow too hard. 'Pocahontas is the friend of Jamestown,' I will call to the sun and it will not beat too fiercely down upon it. 'Pocahontas loves Jamestown,' I shall whisper to the river and it will not flood the island's banks and—" Here, Pocahontas's voice grew more serious and intense. "Most important of all," she continued, "I who sit close to Powhatan's heart shall whisper every day in his ear, 'If you love Matoaka, do not harm Jamestown.' "

A look of great relief passed over the wounded man's face. Pocahontas had been able to do what no colonist could: soothe his anxieties and calm his soul.

"I thank you again, little sister," he said, pausing. "And now bid me farewell, for here come the sailors to carry me to the ship."

Pocahontas sprang up and bending over him, whispered tender

Indian words of farewell. Then, as the sailors approached, she fled toward the gates and into the forest without looking back.

And as the ship sailed slowly away from Jamestown, John Smith thought he caught sight of a white buckskin skirt between the trees.

He rested his head on the pillow and let the lapping waters lull him to sleep. "Good-bye, Pocahontas," he murmured. "Good-bye, my dear friend."

CHAPTER 16

CAPTAIN ARGALL TAKES A PRISONER

Three years passed and not one word did Pocahontas hear from Captain John Smith. But she never forgot him. She thought about him every day.

In the beginning, she made trips to Jamestown quite frequently, remembering the promise she had made to him to help Jamestown during the "starving time" of winter. She brought corn and grain, seeds and berries, venison and rabbit. Her aid literally kept the colonists alive and she knew that, somewhere, Captain Smith knew what she had done and was smiling on her even from far away.

But things soon began to change. In the year 1610, relations between Powhatan and the colonists turned hostile. They were two very different cultures, and try as they might, they could not find a common basis for understanding. The colonists still considered the Indians "savages" because they did not read or write or attend church. The Indians, in turn, found the colonists strange because they did not understand nature and they could not survive without their magic guns. Anger erupted into skirmishes; fights became battles; people were killed.

Powhatan and his tribe were openly hostile to the colonists. They refused to trade with them any longer. The colonists, for their part, kept trying to force the Indians to trade. But their strong-arm tactics only made the Indians more stubborn.

Even Pocahontas had begun to lose faith. Why had Captain Smith not written to her? Her worse fears were realized when an armed confrontation took place between Captain Ratcliffe, a newcomer to Jamestown, and the Powhatan tribe. Many Englishmen were killed; those taken prisoner reported that Captain John Smith had died in England.

Pocahontas could hardly bear her grief. It pained her so to think that her "brother" was dead, that she would never see him again. She spent much time in the woods, alone, chanting softly by the river.

Suddenly, Jamestown seemed alien and insignificant to her, especially when the colonists retaliated for the dead among Ratcliffe's men with brutal killings of their own. Pocahontas began to believe that these new palefaces were very unlike her "brother." They were not kind or gentle. They did not deserve her help.

She stopped going to Jamestown—starvation once again descended on the colony. By the winter of 1610, there were only sixty members of the original colony still alive.

What Pocahontas did not know was that politics were despoiling the friendship between Jamestown and her people. Ratcliffe was envious of Smith's relationship with the Indians. It was he who spread the rumor that Smith was dead, when, in reality, he was still very much alive, recovering from his wound. Worse, in a proclamation that he sent to the king by boat, Ratcliffe accused Smith of wanting to marry the young Pocahontas, "thereby

becoming king of the New World upon Powhatan's death."
Smith refuted these claims in the London courts, but he felt it
best that he remain aloof from Pocahontas, that he not write her
even one single note.

It was in this climate of despair and hostility that Captain
Argall sailed his ships into Jamestown—and changed the course
of history.

It was a miracle from the sea. Sixty starving settlers stared at the
billowing white sails moving toward them like clouds on the water. Captain Argall had brought supplies with him: food, cooking
pots, hunting knives, and building materials. But in a few weeks'
time, the food supply had dwindled once again and now there
were even more people who felt the growl of hunger in their
empty stomachs.

Trade with Chief Powhatan had deteriorated to the point that
any attempt at bartering would be fruitless. So Captain Argall,
with Captain Ratcliffe's blessing, attempted to build a relationship with the neighboring Patowomeke tribe. They were cousins
to the Powhatans, but they seemed friendly and they were curious
about the settlers—perhaps even enough so to do business.

As Argall and his men prepared for their journey to the
Patowomeke village, Pocahontas herself was planning her own
visit to her cousins. She had not seen them for a long time and
she was feeling restless—especially now that Claw-of-the-Eagle
was paying her much unwanted attention.

It had begun several moons earlier. Claw-of-the-Eagle had become a full-fledged member of his adopted tribe after his courage
and endurance had been tested in numerous skirmishes with the
palefaces. Chief Powhatan himself had praised his deeds during
council meetings. Claw-of-the-Eagle had hated the white men

from the beginning, and he had never approved of the friendship between Pocahontas and John Smith. The fact was that Claw-of-the-Eagle was in love with Pocahontas.

One day old Wansutis said to him, "My son, it is time now for you to marry. My hands grow weak, and a young wife would be a better partner than I. You need to share your life with someone who will grow old with you." She exhaled a puff of smoke from her pipe and raised her face to the sun. "Look around you, my son, and choose."

Claw-of-the-Eagle had long been thinking that the time *had* come to marry, but he had no need to look about and choose. He had made his choice long ago, and, even though she was the daughter of the great Powhatan, he did not doubt that the chief would give her to one of his best braves. And so, one evening in *taquitock*, or autumn, when the red glow of the leaves was veiled by an early frost, Claw-of-the-Eagle took his flute and went to find Pocahontas.

Not far from her wigwam, he seated himself on a stone and began to play the plaintive song in which an Indian brave tells of his longing for the maiden he would make his wife.

"Do you hear that, Pocahontas?" asked Cleopatra, who had peeked out through the wigwam covering. "It is Claw-of-the-Eagle. He plays for you. Go to him, Sister, and make his heart glad, for there is no other brave who can compare to him."

"I will not be his wife," replied Pocahontas. "Go yourself if he pleases you so much." She refused to stir from her tent all that evening, even though the gentle music continued until well after the moon rose.

But Claw-of-the-Eagle did not despair. He played his music night after night. After all, he had always been a successful hunter. He had never come back to Wansutis's lodge empty-handed. He had never failed in any quest. And he did not mean to fail now.

So, even when Pocahontas left Werowocomoco to visit her cousins, he bided his time. He spent his days building a beautiful new lodge so it would be ready for the day when he brought Pocahontas home as his wife and they lit their first fire beneath the opening under the sky.

Pocahontas soon settled in with her cousins. The Patowomekes had always been generous, especially their chief, Japezaws. He and his family made sure that Pocahontas had fresh straw and skins for her sleeping pallet. They served venison, sweet apples, and corn at almost every meal. They asked her to join in their dances and council meetings.

So Pocahontas was with the Patowomekes when Captain Argall's ship sailed to their shore.

Japezaws received the captain in a friendly manner. "Yes," he said, "we will sell you corn as I sold it to your great Captain Smith when he first came among us. What news have you of him? Will he come again to us? He was a great brave."

"We have no word from him," Captain Argall answered. "It is possible that the stories are true, that he might be dead." And then, because he, too, was jealous of Smith's fame among the Indians, he felt compelled to add, "England has so many great braves that we waste little thought on those who are gone. Jamestown has all but forgotten him already."

"There is one among us who forgets him not," said Japezaws, pointing to his village in the valley behind him. "There is one who has him and his deeds always in her thoughts."

"Who might that be?" asked Argall, wondering if the Patowomekes held an Englishman captive.

"It is his friend, Pocahontas, who grieves for him and still hopes that he is alive, that he will return. She is our cousin, and has come to stay with us, as she has grown restless since she heard the tales about Smith."

As Japezaws spoke, a thought arose in Argall's mind. And, in the time it took Japezaws's braves to carry corn and dried meat to the ship, the Englishman had formed a plan.

"I wish, Chief Japezaws," he began, "that Chief Powhatan, the father of Pocahontas, had as great a love for Jamestown as his daughter. He will not sell provisions to us, even though his store house is full to overflowing. It is only a matter of a few more harvests before we have food to spare," Argall said, gesturing to his great ship, "but where will he find such copper kettles, such mirrors, such knives of bright steel as we would pay him now in exchange for that which he has in plenty?"

The old chief's eyes glistened with greed. "But I would have some shining knives," he said. "I wish to see a kettle that will not break when it falls on a rock. I want some of the marvels you keep in your lodges."

Argall smiled. "Well, as soon as your warriors can travel to Jamestown and back, they will be yours." The captain paused. "That is," and he coughed, "if you will do what I ask."

"And what is that?" asked Japezaws with suspicion.

"It is simple enough. Listen," continued Argall, warming to his plan. "You know about the enmity between ourselves and Chief Powhatan. But," Argall paused again, not wanting to sound too eager, "but, if we held someone hostage who was dear to Powhatan, we could force him to trade with us. We could force him to make peace with us."

Argall glanced at Japezaws, but he could not tell his reaction. He decided to continue nonetheless. "If you will entrust the Princess Pocahontas to us," he went on, "we will take her to Jamestown where she will be treated as a most important guest until

Chief Powhatan agrees to our terms. At that time, we will take her safely back to her father."

Argall took off his plumed hat and nervously fanned his sweating face. At any point, Japezaws could become very angry and Argall could lose the precious friendship he had forged with this tribe—and fail in his plan to hold Pocahontas hostage. He took a deep breath and plunged on. "And, for your help in this matter, you will receive magnificent presents such as you have never seen, gifts that no one, not even Powhatan, has ever received."

Japezaws was silent as he thought the matter over. Pocahontas was his relative as well as his guest, and his people had always upheld the sacred duties of hospitality. But he also knew that no harm would befall her. The friendship the English felt toward her was well known to all his tribe, as was the great affection her father felt for his favorite daughter. In a day or two, she would be ransomed by Chief Powhatan, and that would be the end of it. Meanwhile, for his part in the matter, he, Japezaws, would get what he so greatly longed to possess. He wasted neither time nor words. "Return to this place at sunset, and I will bring her to you."

Claw-of-the-Eagle had finished building the new lodge for his wife-to-be. He had hunted and fished and there was nothing for which he needed to leave Werowocomoco. He could stay and keep Wansutis company, dreaming about Pocahontas while he made a new, strong bow and some arrows.

But, suddenly, in the midst of grinding corn into meal, Wansutis looked up as if she heard voices. Her grinding stone fell to the earth as she grabbed Claw-of-the-Eagle's arm and said calmly, "My son, if your mind is truly set upon a certain maiden for your wife, go seek her at once in the village of the Patowomekes. She is in danger."

"No, no," cried Pocahontas. "You must not go."
Page 134

"Do not shoot!"
Page 154

Although Claw-of-the-Eagle had heard nothing, he knew enough not to ask his mother for explanations. He had learned long ago that she seemed to possess magical powers he could never understand, but which he respected. Thus, without any discussion, and with only a word of farewell, he took his bow and arrows and his flute, and quickly set forth for the Patowomeke village.

After traveling for several days, he approached their village, filled with resolve. "Before three days have passed," he said to himself, "I shall return this way with my wife. No longer will I wait for her. She will listen to my music and be mine, for I know she is fond of me, too."

Knowing that he was approaching a friendly allied tribe, Claw-of-the-Eagle strode along as openly and as carelessly as he would have done at Werowocomoco. But, suddenly, like a deer that scents a bear, he stood still, his nostrils quivering. He slipped behind a tree and notched an arrow to his bow.

A white man, he thought, long before his eyes caught sight of him.

Concealed by the tree, he waited, and watched the man pass. He recognized him as the new English captain, but, to his astonishment, he saw that the women who were walking with him were Pocahontas and the wife of Japezaws.

"As someone who has seen the things in the lodges of the palefaces firsthand, can you blame me for my eagerness to see them as well?" Japezaws's wife was saying to Pocahontas, as she passed by the tree where Claw-of-the-Eagle hid. "Is it right for you to be surprised that I am eager to see with my own eyes such strange ways as theirs, and the marvels the white chief has stored in the canoe?"

"Of course not," laughed Pocahontas, "and, in truth, I am glad to go with you to translate your questions with the few words of their tongue that I have not forgotten. I, too, have questions to ask Captain Argall. And I, too, would like to see the white man's marvels once again!"

After they had passed, the young brave followed after, far enough behind that Pocahontas's sharp ear could not hear his step.

At the bank where the English boat was moored, Claw-of-the-Eagle sought cover behind a large boulder, his eyes never moving from the women before him. He watched them go on board and saw the English sailors rise to greet them. He heard the eager exclamations of Japezaws's wife as she felt their clothes and touched the objects on the deck of the boat. Pocahontas explained as best she could about the anchor and sails, about cooking utensils and muskets. Claw-of-the-Eagle then saw Captain Argall open a small chest and hand the two women some bright beads and lace handkerchiefs as Japezaws's wife once again uttered cries of delight.

Claw-of-the-Eagle waited to see what would happen next. After an hour, he saw the two women approach the side of the boat nearest the shore, the older one in front. She jumped to the bank and ran quickly off into the forest. Pocahontas had one foot out of the boat, ready to follow, when Captain Argall took hold of her arm.

"Come with us to Jamestown, Princess," he said. "We would welcome you for a visit."

Pocahontas's anger flared. Never in her life had she been restrained by force. She wasted neither time nor strength in entreaty, but, instead, tried to wrench herself away from him. The Englishman held her firmly, but gently, and, while she struggled, the sailors shoved the boat out into the stream.

Claw-of-the Eagle immediately rose from behind the boulder. He aimed and shot at the Englishman. The arrow struck the surprised captain on his leather vest, but it did no more than knock the wind out of him.

"Shoot into the trees there," Argall commanded, still holding Pocahontas.

One of the sailors aimed toward the thicket at his still-invisible enemy, when Claw-of-the-Eagle realized that the boat was rapidly swinging out of his range. He ran out onto an exposed bluff and readied another arrow. However, before it left his bow, the soldier fired his musket and a bullet hit the brave in the shoulder. As Claw-of-the-Eagle fell, Pocahontas uttered a cry of horror. At that moment, she had seen the face of her wounded defender.

CHAPTER 17

Pocahontas Loses a Friend

It was the second night of Pocahontas's captivity. She was loosely restrained on deck—just what was necessary to keep her from jumping overboard. Argall and the sailors treated her with great deference. But Pocahontas was very lonely and unhappy. In her life she had always been free to come and go and it was almost a physical pain for her to be imprisoned within the narrow limits of the boat. Several times she had tried to evade the watchful eyes of the sailors, but her cunning, so superior in the woods, was useless on this unfamiliar boat.

Her anger at Japezaws and his wife flamed anew every time she thought about their treachery. She thought often about what kind of punishment she would beg her father to inflict upon them, and of the honor he should bestow to Claw-of-the-Eagle. In fact, she had decided that she would marry Claw-of-the-Eagle when she returned home. He was a brave man and she knew he loved her very much.

148

"Wait!" she shouted as she stood looking over the stern in the direction of the Patowomeke village, her eyes flashing. "Wait until you are brought to my father to be tortured!"

Seeing the bewildered faces of her cousins and knowing they could not understand her, Pocahontas sighed. She sat back on the deck, leaning on the stern and thinking about Claw-of-the-Eagle. Was he lying dead in the forest? What a friend and companion he had always been, she thought, how brave, how strong! She was afraid to think that he might be dead. Better to imagine him following the boat through the silent forest along the riverbank, waiting for the right moment to save her.

By nightfall of the second day, the boat was anchored in the center of a stream that widened into a small bay. Captain Argall, who had not known what to make of Claw-of-the-Eagle's attack, was uneasy. He was not certain that Japezaws had not betrayed him. He therefore made as much speed as possible that first night and the following day. Now his weary men needed rest and, as there appeared to be no sign of pursuit, he had allowed them to get some sleep. Only one sailor was left on watch, but he, too, was tired, and kept drifting off to sleep.

Pocahontas lay alone in the stern, her head pillowed on a roll of sailcloth. Argall had done everything he could to make her comfortable, and he never spoke to her unless he first bowed low, his hat in hand. Now she, too, had fallen asleep, her eyes wet with the tears she would not shed in the daylight. She dreamed she was again at Werowocomoco and that she had just risen from her sleeping mat to run out into the moonlight as she had done so often.

Suddenly, something awakened her, a faint sound scarcely louder than the lapping of the water against the side of the boat. She opened her eyes but did not move, and waited, tense with excitement. A fish flopped out of the water, and then all was silent again. She closed her heavy eyes once more. Then it came again, no louder than the wind in the pine trees on the shore: "Pocahontas!"

Raising herself to her elbow with a motion as quiet as a cat's, she peered into the dark water over the stern. A hand came out of the darkness and clasped her wrist. She did not need to see the features of the face below her to know whose it was.

"Claw-of-the-Eagle," she whispered, "is it really you? I was afraid the white man's gun had killed you, and I have been so sad."

"I lay still for an hour," he answered softly, as he lifted himself up in the water and hung with both hands to the side of the boat. "But I was wounded only on the shoulder and not on the leg. Stiffness has made me slow, like a bear that has been hurt in a trap. But I put mud on the wound and wrapped it with my leggings, and I have followed close behind you from along the shore."

"I knew you would come after me if you were not dead," she whispered.

"Yes, I have come for you, Pocahontas," he said, and there was grown-up firmness in the youth's voice. "Waste no time. Drop down here beside me as quietly as if you were stalking a deer. We will swim underwater until we are beyond reach of the white men's dull ears and, before three days have passed, we shall be once again at your father's lodge."

The thought of all that home meant made Pocahontas pause. The affection of her father and brothers, the haunts in the forest and on the river, the freedom of her daily existence—here was her chance to return to them. If she did not take it, what lay ahead for her? A terror of the unknown overcame her for the first time. The knowledge that an old and loyal friend was near was as welcome as a light shining in a dark night. And yet she answered, "I cannot go with you, Claw-of-the-Eagle."

The young brave uttered a low murmur of astonishment. "Do you not realize," he asked, "that Japezaws has betrayed you, that you are to be kept captive in Jamestown in order to force Chief Powhatan to do whatever the English desire of him?"

Pocahontas slowly nodded. "Yes, I know. Captain Argall has told me all."

"And yet still you hesitate? Are you, the daughter of a mighty chief, *afraid* to attempt escape?"

She did not lower herself to reply to such a charge, but whispered instead, "Had you come last night, I would have gone with you only too gladly. In truth, I had decided to escape myself tonight, no matter what the difficulties might be. I have a knife and know how to use it. But during the night I came to think otherwise, for there have been long hours in which to think. You know that captivity is as terrible to me as to a wild dove. But as I sat here alone with nothing to do, I followed a trail in my mind that led only to Jamestown, and so I am going there."

"But why?" asked Claw-of-the-Eagle.

"Because by going, I believe I can serve both our nation and the English," Pocahontas whispered. She gulped and bit her lip; the words she spoke took great courage. "My brother, John Smith, said we must be friends, and I promised him, before he left, to watch over the welfare of his people. My father loves me so much that in order to free me I think he will do as the English wish, and so I will go with Captain Argall in the hope that peace will come again between our two peoples. But," and her voice rose so much that Claw-of-the-Eagle tightened his hold on her hand to remind her of their danger. "But," she continued in a lower voice, "I will not intercede for that traitor Japezaws and his crafty wife. My father may wreak vengeance on them as he will."

Her voice, low as it was, had risen again with her emotion, and the boy's keen hearing had caught the movement of a man's foot on the wooden deck. They became still for a moment. When all was quiet again, Claw-of-the-Eagle asked sadly, in a tone that sounded as mournful as wind in the pine trees, "Then you will not come with me? I built a lodge for you, Matoaka, with a smoke hole wide enough to let in the whole moon. My arrows have killed deer and turkeys for you and I have smoked and hung meat that would last us through the whole winter."

Claw-of-the-Eagle sighed deeply. He stretched an arm over the rim of the boat and gently touched Pocahontas's cheek. "A young woman and a young brave need to be together. I came to Japezaws's village to sing this to you. Now I have run wounded through the forests and swum the black stream to tell it to you and yet you bid me turn back alone." Claw-of-the-Eagle shook his wet head. "If you have no wish to enter my lodge, let me at least escort you safely to your father."

"I thank you, Claw-of-the-Eagle, for all you have done," Pocahontas whispered, "and all you would do for me." She gazed into the young man's eyes, brilliant in the moonlight. "There is no braver warrior in all the tribes. But I have listened to my spirit guide and it has said to me, 'Remember the word you gave your white brother.'"

Claw-of-the-Eagle knew that it was useless to plead, and yet he could not help himself. "Come back with me, Matoaka. Please. What are the white men to you and me?"

But she only whispered, "Go, Claw-of-the-Eagle, go quickly before the sailors awake. Go back to old Wansutis so she can bind up your wound. Go tell Chief Powhatan that he must buy my freedom from the English by returning their prisoners and giving them food."

While she spoke, the young brave thought swiftly. The respect he owed Pocahontas as the daughter of the great Chief Powhatan made him believe, at first, that he must do her bidding and leave her. Little by little, however, he began to think of her as a girl, strong and courageous, but completely misguided. He now hated the English more than ever and Pocahontas's promise to aid them seemed to him complete foolishness. Let them all perish on their island or return across the sea from where they had come! Why should she go with them? Why should he let her go? Who knew what treatment she would receive away from her own people? If he rescued her and brought her back to her father, would he not win great favor in the eyes of Chief Powhatan—who then could not refuse to let her be his wife? Feeling resolute, Claw-of-the-Eagle decided that if Pocahontas would not come willingly, he would carry her off against her will, for her own good.

He would rescue Pocahontas and kill the hated white men, too! Had they not wounded him and kidnapped her? There were not many of them and they were all asleep. While he and Pocahontas were talking, he had pulled himself out of the water and thrown his legs over the side of the boat. Now he rose and whispered, "Before I go, I want to know what their canoe is like. Do not be afraid for me. There is no danger. But do not stir."

Pocahontas warned him to leave quickly, for safety's sake, but Claw-of-the-Eagle was already a few paces ahead of her, treading as lightly as if the deck were gravel that would roll about and betray him with its noise. She did not dare call out to him and wake the Englishmen. She saw him draw near to a sleeping sailor and stoop. But it was too dark for her to see that he had stabbed the man in the heart.

The sailor died instantly and Claw-of-the-Eagle moved softly on to the next sailor.

Pocahontas sensed that something strange was happening.

Claw-of-the-Eagle was taking too long to look at a mere canoe, but she dared not go in search of him and cause him trouble.

The second and third sailors were killed as easily as the first. Already the dawn was coming and the young brave could distinguish the forms of four other men. He bent over one of them. His hand shaking from excitement and from the fever brought on by his wound, accidentally touched the man's cheek. The sailor immediately cried out and Claw-of-the-Eagle, realizing that he had been discovered, slashed out with his knife as he ran for the stern.

He could have leapt overboard easily and escaped, but though he had failed to kill all his enemies, he wanted to rescue Pocahontas. He dashed toward her, followed by the sailor. Roused by the outcry, Argall and the two remaining crewmen were at their heels. Claw-of-the-Eagle caught Pocahontas in his arms and before she could resist, he had jumped with her into the river.

The sailor, who had only been slightly wounded by the young brave's knife, seized his musket as he ran. "Do not shoot!" Argall called out breathlessly. He did not know what had happened, but he did know that Pocahontas was gone. "The Indian princess is there in the water. Do not shoot, for the love of heaven, or we shall have all the Indians in America after us!"

The sailor however, had already made out the two figures in the water, so close together that Argall's older eyes had seen them as one. And just as Claw-of-the-Eagle, hampered by his wounded shoulder, was about to sink below the surface to swim under water, the sailor took aim. The bullet hit the top of the young man's head, gashing his skin.

Pocahontas saw that Claw-of-the-Eagle was not badly wounded, but the blood running down his face and into his mouth and nose made it impossible for him to breathe deeply enough to swim underwater. The weakness caused by his other wound also made his motions slower. Before he would be able to put a safe distance between himself and the boat, the sailor would have fired again.

Pocahontas realized, however, he would not fire at her.

With a few rapid strokes, she had reached her friend and had slipped her arm under his wounded shoulder, bearing him up.

"Now, Claw-of-the-Eagle," she cried, "let us make for the shore. They will not dare fire at me."

Argall and his men watched their hostage and her rescuer make their escape, powerless to prevent it. Though Claw-of-the-Eagle's strokes grew slower and slower, Pocahontas's strength kept him afloat. Once on shore, the Englishmen knew, the two would be able to hide so that no white man could hope to find them. And it was more than likely that other Indians might be lurking in the forest.

"Fooled! Fooled!" cried out Argall, hitting one fist against the other in vexation.

But the man who had wounded Claw-of-the-Eagle was not one who willingly gave up a chase. His forebears had been outlaws with Robin Hood, skillful archers and bowmen with Henry V at Agincourt, whose arrows never failed to find French marks. The same keen eye and strong arm were his with a musket. He saw that the two Indians had reached a willow tree with roots that lay twisted about each other across the surface of the river. For one second the youth and the maiden, close together, hung on to this natural shelf, gaining the strength to pull themselves up onto the ground. He realized how disastrous it would be to injure the daughter of Chief Powhatan. Nevertheless, he was determined to take a chance.

To the horror of his captain, he took careful aim and fired. This time the bullet found its mark. It hit the young brave squarely in the head and killed him.

Horrified, Pocahontas tried to catch Claw-of-the-Eagle in her arms before his body sank heavily into the water and disappeared without a sound. Dead! Gone! And so quickly! The boy who had been her friend, who had tried to save her!

Pocahontas could not weep as she floated along with no conscious movement. Then, slowly and deliberately, she turned and swam back toward the boat. The sailors wondered in amazement if she really was returning to them. She let herself be helped over the side by Captain Argall.

"I will go with you to Jamestown now" was all she said. She gave no explanation of what had happened and she refused to answer any questions or tell the English why she had chosen to go with them when she could have been free.

After a brief funeral service for their dead comrades, they hoisted the anchor and started off. The sun was rising but the air was still cold and the sailors brought their dry coats to Pocahontas to keep her warm. They gave her food but she would not touch it, nor would she speak, nor turn her face from the river.

As they began to sail slowly downstream, Pocahontas leaned back over the gunwale and saw the body of Claw-of-the-Eagle, borne by a swift eddy, float by her. She rose to her feet and, with the light of the sun falling upon her face and her uplifted arms, she sang aloud the song of death as her people sang it, strong and true, while the river hurried with its burden toward the sea.

CHAPTER 18

A BAPTISM IN JAMESTOWN

Pocahontas thought only of Claw-of-the-Eagle during the journey to Jamestown. She stared out at the water, barely speaking and barely eating, thinking about the way he played his flute, his bravery in battle, his ready smile. She missed her people with an ache that would not go away: her brother Nautauquas; her sister Cleopatra; her father; and even old Wansutis. She wished she were back in her lodge, sitting by the fire, with the good scents of the earth mingling with those of smoking meat and burning pine logs, and with the moon a showing perfect circle in the opening at the top of the lodge.

Pocahontas sighed. The die was cast and her destiny—Jamestown—awaited.

News of the group's imminent arrival had preceded them, and the entire settlement had turned out at the wharf to greet them. Captain Argall stepped ashore. "I have brought back a good supply of food from the Patowomekes," he reported, "and something of far greater value: Princess Pocahontas, the daughter of Chief Powhatan." With that, he helped the poised young woman out of the boat.

A council member, in his best purple vest and new dark-red leather boots, came forward, doffing his plumed hat. "Welcome, Princess," he said, bowing. "Do not be angry with us if we, in all courtesy, ask you to stay with us for a while. We hope it will please you to visit us again, to stay for a few days with those who have been in your debt ever since you saved the life of Captain John Smith."

Pocahontas had been prepared to show her anger at the treachery of Japezaws and Argall; she had been feeling uncooperative and resentful. But the name of Captain John Smith disarmed her. She remembered the promise she had made to her white brother before he had returned to England.

Pocahontas felt that she must keep her word. She would continue to show friendship toward Jamestown, just as she had always done. So she smiled at the councilman and greeted those whom she knew. She let the settlers guide her to the house where she would be staying. Mrs. Lettice, the wife of one of the colonists, was to stay there with her, as much for company as to keep watch over her. Mrs. Lettice had laid out some of her own clothing in case the Indian maiden wanted to change. And Pocahontas, distracted from the dangers and sadness of the past few days, laughed with amusement as she tried on the petticoats and full yellow skirts.

"They are sending messengers to your father, King Powhatan," the Englishwoman said, as she showed Pocahontas how to arrange a starched collar; it scratched her neck so much that she grimaced. Mrs. Lettice, caught up in her own important role, did not notice Pocahontas's expression and chattered on. "They will tell him that you are here, and I am sure that in his anxiety to see you again, he will give us whatever we demand: our men, the arms they have taken, a good supply of corn."

Mrs. Lettice fluffed the sleeves on Pocahontas's blouse, pausing as she thought about the best way to enlist the princess's help. "Perhaps you would like to send some word of your own to your father," she suggested. "There is an Indian boy here at the settlement who has brought fish to trade. He can take a message to your father."

"Bring him to me, please," Pocahontas said, slowly pronouncing the English words she had not spoken in so long.

She was looking at herself in an ebony-framed mirror that hung opposite the door, staring at her strange appearance, when Mrs. Lettice entered the room with the Indian boy. Pocahontas saw the boy's face in the glass and recognized him as the son of another Powhatan chief. She turned and faced him, suddenly realizing that he did not know who she was. He saw only her English clothes and so believed her to be an Englishwoman. This amused Pocahontas. She could not wait to see his reaction when she revealed to him who she was.

"Little Squirrel!" she exclaimed, laughing. The boy's mouth opened in shock. "Matoaka?"

"Yes!" Pocahontas said, turning around to show off her wide-hooped skirt. "It is I!"

Pocahontas grew serious. "Take this sad message to old Wan-sutis when you return to our village," she said gravely. "Tell her that her son, Claw-of-the-Eagle, has met his death bravely and that Pocahontas mourns him with her."

She lowered her head and paused. Her sorrow made her feel old beyond her years. She then dismissed Little Squirrel.

As he walked away, she remembered something else she wanted to tell him, but the unaccustomed weight of her clothes and the awkwardness of the English shoes prevented her from reaching the boy in time. In frustration, Pocahontas stomped back to the house, and began to pull off the cumbersome clothes. "No, I will not imprison myself in these garments," she cried. "Give me back my own things!" She breathed deeply with satisfaction as she pulled up her leggings and tied her buckskin skirt around her body.

Had Pocahontas come to Jamestown under different circumstances, she might have enjoyed seeing her English friends again. It had been a long time since her last visit, and everything seemed new and exciting. But now she was there under duress— and she had suffered the grievous loss of a dear friend along the way. She could feel no joy, no happiness. She felt only impatience as she counted the days, the hours, the minutes until the messengers returned from Werowocomoco with the news that her father had met the demands of the English and she could go home.

But things did not go as Pocahontas had hoped. The very next day, while Pocahontas fretted in her English lodging, dreaming of the forest and her family, the messengers arrived with unexpected news. The English captives had been returned, but Powhatan had refused to give up all the muskets he had taken or send the bushels of corn—not until his daughter was returned safely to his side.

And so the talks continued—day after day of negotiating and compromising. But neither white man nor Indian was satisfied, and Pocahontas, the valuable hostage, remained at Jamestown, while weeks turned into months.

Although she was frustrated that an agreement could not be reached, Pocahontas was slowly adapting to her new life. She could not help herself: her optimistic nature, her enthusiasm, and her natural curiosity overcame her hostility. And the English treated her with such great courtesy that she found it difficult to remember that she was a captive. She was welcomed into every house, where she ate from flat bowls called dishes, drank wine from goblets, and wiped her face afterward with a cloth. She loved the bright flowers that graced the table in the great house built for the governor of Jamestown. And she asked endless questions of everyone.

"How do you fire a musket?"

"How do you tie a corset?"

"Why do you remove your hat and bow to me?"

Pocahontas was especially taken with letter writing. She was fascinated by the wax the colonists used to seal their letters. She loved the intricate design of the great red seal that Master John Rolfe, Secretary and Recorder General of the colony, affixed to every document that went by sea to London.

For his part, John Rolfe was equally fascinated with Pocahontas. He patiently answered all her questions, and felt great pleasure each time her dark eyes brightened with comprehension. He enjoyed her visits to the boring Council meetings, finding her laughter and bright manner a welcome change from the somber manner of the Council members.

John Rolfe was a widower and, although he had recovered from the loss of his beloved wife, he missed a woman's companionship —and he found himself thinking a great deal about the Indian princess. So, when she asked him to accompany her around Jamestown and answer her questions, he was not at all averse to doing so.

"I have more questions than the nuts a squirrel stores in winter," Pocahontas told him. "Listen. What keeps your ships from sailing away with the tide? Why do you use coins in your store? Where did you get the feather for your hat?" One after the other, the questions came, including the one about the man imprisoned for theft in the wooden stocks that stood in the village square.

And Rolfe found himself enjoying every single minute he spent in Pocahontas's company.

And he was not the only one: Pocahontas found herself enjoying the afternoons she spent with him, strolling around the settlement, laughing, and talking to the colonists as if she were one of them.

In fact, Pocahontas felt so comfortable that she even began to tease John Rolfe the same way she had so long ago teased her brother or Claw-of-the-Eagle. "Would you like to try a persimmon?" she asked Rolfe one day, picking the golden fruit from a nearby tree. It looked delicious and Rolfe was pleased to try the exotic fruit. But Pocahontas could barely suppress a mischievous smile; she knew that the fruit was not yet ripe—and that it would be extremely sour. She laughed and laughed as he bit into the juicy fruit, his lips puckering as he spit it out.

"Ow!" he said, but there was laughter in his eyes. "I shall pay you back for this someday," he teased when he was able to speak again.

But as comfortable as John Rolfe made her feel, he was not Captain John Smith. Pocahontas missed Smith more than she ever had, especially now, when she was living among his people. Although she had heard, when she was in Werowocomoco, that he had died, some of the colonists had heard rumors from London that he was still alive. Others had heard that he had gone to Turkey and was fighting the heathens in a religious crusade. Still others said that he had grown fat and lazy in England and there were yet others who claimed he would be returning to Jamestown on the very next ship.

Whatever the truth was, the mere fact that John Smith might be alive brought Pocahontas new, burgeoning hope, and made her stay in Jamestown that much more bearable. She dreamed that she saw his ship enter the inlet, its white sails billowing in the wind. In the dream she saw him at the stern, waving his powerful arms in greeting. And she saw herself running to the ship as it anchored, flying to her white brother and embracing him as if she would never let him go. He would smooth her hair and hold her close, pleased that she had kept her promise, that she had made sure that Jamestown survived.

But, always, at the moment that John Smith smiled down at her, the dream evaporated, and Pocahontas would wake to find herself alone, lying on an English bed, enclosed in a house that kept out the sounds and the peace of the outdoors.

She would sigh then, and tell herself to be content to learn as much as she could about the English and their customs. As the weeks passed, she became more and more dependent on John Rolfe for that education.

As summer turned into the autumn of 1612, Pocahontas found herself still at Jamestown, and more and more drawn to the settlement's church. The white structure with its tower intrigued her. She was fascinated by the clanging bells that called the people of Jamestown to daily prayers. They seemed to speak a language she could not understand. Nor could she understand the ceremony that she observed, wide-eyed, in which the white-robed clergyman stretched out his arms over the men and women of the colony, as they kneeled before him.

"What does it mean?" she asked, and Rolfe tried to explain the mysteries of his faith to her. He had a vested interest in helping Pocahontas understand the ways of the English church. As a devout Puritan, he knew he could marry only someone who professed the same Christian faith. But he was thinking more and more about Pocahontas and he knew he was growing to love her. How could he marry her, a heathen from the New World? Rolfe knew it would be possible only if Pocahontas were baptized a Christian. But he was not a clergyman and he felt it would be too difficult for him to explain the tenets of his religion properly, so he requested of the Reverend Thomas Alexander Whitaker that he step in to instruct Pocahontas in the ways of the Church of England.

This the zealous and gentle minister gladly consented to do. Here was the great opportunity he had hoped for since coming to Virginia—to make an Indian convert so notable that the conversion would bring others in its wake. And what finer convert could there be than the Indian princess herself!

But it would not be an easy task. Pocahontas's knowledge of English did not extend beyond the simplest expressions. Reverend Whitaker nearly despaired of making her understand all the intricacies of the Gospel. However, he need not have worried. The stories of the Bible held Pocahontas spellbound—as did the colorful pictures illustrating religious themes he showed her in heavy leatherbound volumes.

"Why do you always put flowers on that table?" she asked the Reverend one day, pointing to the vases of fresh blossoms on the altar. "What good does your god receive from them?"

The Reverend thought for a moment. He and Pocahontas were sitting in the cool shade of the dark church, looking out the open door at the swaying branches of the trees and the river beyond. He finally said, "Do you not take delight in the sunshine, Princess? I have seen you lift up your arms toward the blue skies and white clouds as if you would embrace the whole wide world. Why do you take pleasure in such things?"

"Because," Pocahontas said, hesitating, as she cast about for an explanation, "because they make me happy."

The Reverend nodded. "And because they are beautiful. And God who created all this beauty rejoices in it too—in the great fields and noble trees, in the strong men and women and happy children. In thanks for all this bounty, we put beautiful flowers on His table."

"Does He delight in evil and torture, too?"

"No," he answered. "Such things are only of the Devil. Our God and our beliefs have to do with beauty and love."

The Reverend gave Pocahontas much to ponder. She found herself drawn to this new religion. Reverend Whitaker's fatherly kindness to her, the colony's acceptance of her, and the fact that her brother, John Smith, believed in this God—all this drew her to the English church.

Pocahontas's religious instruction lasted several weeks, until, at last, Reverend Whitaker believed the Indian princess was ready and willing to be baptized.

The governor, Sir Thomas Dale, was pleased to hear the news. When, by chance, he met Pocahontas at the wharf, watching sailors unload a ship that had just arrived from England, he bowed and greeted her with a smile. "We are so pleased that you have chosen to let go of your heathen ways and embrace the devout ways of our God through baptism," he said. "You will be very happy as a Christian—as are we all."

"I have not given up my people!" Pocahontas cried angrily. "I am not a heathen. I, too, have a god—Okee—whom I pray to. And my people have harvests and trees and beauty for which we give thanks to our Great Spirit. Our ways are good, too, and beautiful!" With that, and to Sir Thomas's amazement, she angrily turned her back and stormed off into a nearby thicket.

She lay down upon the ground, panting with emotion, her thoughts spinning. "Why should I forsake the god of my fathers?" she wondered. "Why should I hate Okee, whom my brothers serve? Why should I prefer this god of the strangers?"

Pocahontas did not understand that her outburst was triggered by a sudden attack of homesickness. How she longed to sit once again at her father's knee, to hunt with Nautauquas, to play with Cleopatra! She felt angry that they had abandoned her to the white men, that her father had not given in to their demands and ransomed her immediately. A whole year had gone by. A whole year!

Pocahontas wondered if her family had stopped caring for her, and if that was why they had left her to remain among the strangers. She began to cry with great, gulping sobs. A river of tears streaked her face and mingled with the earth.

It was here in the woods, at sunset, that Reverend Whitaker found her. An astonished Sir Thomas had related to him what had happened and, in his wisdom, the Reverend had understood that Pocahontas was homesick for her old way of life—and scared of her future as a Christian.

He did not attempt to convince her right away that she should be baptized. The clergyman continued instead to explain gently that he believed Pocahontas had been given a gift, one that she could share with her Indian brothers and sisters—the gift of God.

By April 1613, Pocahontas had faced her fears and decided that to become a Christian was the right thing for her to do. So, one lovely spring day, dressed in a simple white gown, free of collars and ruffles, with her long black hair hanging down her back, Pocahontas entered Jamestown's little church. It was filled to capacity with all the settlers—and even a few Indians from the mainland who were puzzled as to what it all meant. And, while the bells rang softly in the warm spring air, Pocahontas became the first of her people to be baptized a Christian. Her new name would be Rebecca.

CHAPTER 19

JOHN ROLFE

The baptism changed Pocahontas's status in the community and her conversion made her more a part of Jamestown than before. She was now called Lady Rebecca, as befitted a princess, and, with her new name, she seemed to assume a new, womanly dignity. She matured.

And to John Rolfe, she seemed to grow more lovely every day. He spent much time with her, strolling all over the island on which Jamestown stood and through the mainland forests. In the woods, Pocahontas taught Rolfe as much as he taught her in town. She showed him how to observe the habits of wild animals and to find his way through a dense, overgrown forest. Sometimes they would fish from one of the small boats or dig for oysters the way Pocahontas had been taught by her people.

Most of the time, Rolfe was very happy in Pocahontas's company, but there were moments when he felt worried and sad. It was a joy for him to be in the company of someone who made him feel the wonder and excitement of life and who showed him how interesting and beautiful the woods, fields, and rivers could be. But when he thought about marriage, he remembered the obstacles that remained and he would grow concerned. Although Pocahontas was a princess, she was still the child of an alien people—and the daughter of a chief who hated the white colonists. And there were also his own people. What would his family and friends say if he, an English gentleman, chose her instead of a woman of his own race, brought up in the same manner as he? And he wondered how he really felt about that, if he had prejudices he had not admitted even to himself.

Then there were also the powerful leaders of both their peoples to contend with. It was unlikely that Chief Powhatan would ever consent to let his daughter wed a white man, or that the governor of Jamestown would allow it. Rolfe went back and forth in his thinking until he was almost dizzy. But no matter what difficulties occurred to him he always returned to the great determination he felt to win Pocahontas's love and marry her. And now that she had become a Christian, there was at least one less significant barrier between them.

Rolfe believed that his feelings for Pocahontas had not yet been noticed by anyone, but Mrs. Lettice, who had grown very fond of the Indian maiden while she had been in her care, was far from blind to what might concern her charge. She also had heard enough of the discussions that had taken place in the Council meetings to know that such a union was highly desirable and would be approved because it would secure the valuable friendship of Chief Powhatan for the colony. But she was also aware of one major obstacle which could prevent its coming to pass. This was something she needed to act on—or the marriage would never take place.

One day, when the oak trees were finally beginning to green and the lilacs were in full bloom, Mrs. Lettice invited certain members of the Council to her house for tea and the ale her brother had sent over from London on the last ship. She had also baked a lemon cake that quickly won the hearts of the Council members who had been eating only plain baker's bread for months.

When Mrs. Lettice knew the men were comfortable and satisfied, she set her plan into action. "Gentlemen," she began, settling into a cushioned high-backed chair. "We must talk about our Lady Rebecca."

The men put down their cups and prepared to listen: this would indeed be an interesting conversation. Mrs. Lettice continued, "We all know how expedient it would be for the colony if Lady Rebecca were to wed one of us. But," and she paused to take a sip of tea for emphasis, "Lady Rebecca will never wed another while she still harbors the thought that Captain Smith is alive and will return."

"What!" exclaimed one of the Council members who did not hold Smith in high regard. "Are the rumors true that John Smith did indeed seduce the young princess!"

"No, no, no," Mrs. Lettice said, emphatically, shaking her head. She put down her teacup. "No!" She paused to regain her composure. She looked at each man, smiled, and said, "Even Lady Rebecca does not know how she feels. If you were to ask her if she loves John Smith, she would not know how to reply. He stands midway between a god and an elder brother—which is what she calls him. But she *is* in love with him, although it might surprise John Smith to hear it said. Everything she has done for us, everything she has learned, she has done for him. Indeed, she even delayed her baptism in the hope that the rumors were true, that Smith was alive and coming on the next ship to Jamestown."

Mrs. Lettice refilled the men's goblets with ale. She cut herself another piece of lemon cake and, after taking a bite, continued with her final, dramatic thrust. "And I know this full well. She will marry no man, not even John Rolfe, until she hears from him or," and here she paused significantly again, "she believes beyond all doubt that Captain John Smith is dead."

Mrs. Lettice took a deep breath. Her speech was finished and she waited for her words to sink in. She bit her lip. She did not wish to hurt Pocahontas; indeed, she loved her like a daughter. But she truly believed that John Rolfe could make her happy, and that he would be a good husband. Even if Smith were not dead, she thought it highly unlikely he would ever return to Jamestown. He would undoubtedly be on to new adventures, new worlds to discover and conquer.

Mrs. Lettice had chosen her guests well. She knew that the councilmen had grown impatient with Powhatan's reluctance to relinquish that which they wanted. They knew that they had kept Pocahontas in Jamestown too long and that Captain Argall's plan, so brilliant a year ago, had proved disastrous. The only way to create better relations between the white men and the Indians would be a union; in the same way that kings and queens from different countries cemented their alliances with marriages, so, too, could Jamestown befriend the Powhatans by way of a wedding between an Indian princess and an English gentleman. What was a small lie in view of that?

One of the men took a sip of ale and spoke. "In truth, we are mightily amazed at your thoughtful and courageous words, Mrs. Lettice."

"Aye!" a second man agreed.

"But," the first speaker continued, "it sometimes takes an objective eye to see what has been in front of our noses all along. Thank you, Mrs. Lettice, for enabling us to see how important

Master Rolfe's courtship of Lady Rebecca is to us and how well it can be consummated in a wedding that would ally our nations."

The guest who disliked John Smith nodded his head. "It is an easy thing to lie and tell our Lady Rebecca that Smith is dead. For all we know, it is the truth. And think of it. A simple half-truth and the fighting between us will end! I would be honored to offer the news."

He put down his empty goblet, and now that business and pleasure were finished, the company rose to leave.

As they were bidding Mrs. Lettice farewell, Pocahontas entered the house. She had been with Rolfe, as Mrs. Lettice well knew, showing him how her people planted tobacco. He had high hopes for this unusual weed and believed he could make his fortune by selling it in England.

Pocahontas looked around her and smiled. As the men bowed to her, she said, "What brings you gentlemen here?" She laughed, mischief in her eyes. "Has Mrs. Lettice become a member of your esteemed Council?"

The men glanced at each other, the question in their eyes. The enemy of John Smith decided the time to speak was now. "We are so sorry, Princess," he said, bowing low so she could not see his face. "We have come with sad and terrible news."

Pocahontas paled. She looked at each man.

The guest continued. "We have received written confirmation regarding the death of your friend, John Smith. We are very sorry."

"Dead?" cried Pocahontas. "He is dead?"

The men, feeling too guilty to speak a lie again, nodded their assent. They thought Pocahontas might break down in tears or run away, as she had done in the past. But, instead, she stood still, as motionless as a statue. They were relieved to slip out the door with muttered words of sympathy.

Even after they had gone, Mrs. Lettice did not detect any sign of sorrow in the princess.

"I was wrong," she said that night to her husband. "She does not care for the captain, after all. She did not shed even one tear."

But Mrs. Lettice did not hear the door unlatch later that night, nor the soft tread of Pocahontas's moccasined feet as she ran down the street to a quiet, secluded spot on the riverbank. Until dawn, she stood on the shore, her heart so heavy she could not contain it under the white man's roof. She stood with her arms extended to the heavens, her face turned unmoving toward the east, toward the sea, toward the land to which John Smith had sailed away. "Brother!" she wailed in the language of her people. "Brother!" she cried in the ancient tongue, calling on Okee to guide him to the happy hunting ground. Only later, as the sun moved higher in the sky, did she pray to her new God to bear his soul to the Christian heaven.

"Amen," she said, and slowly turning from the sea, she returned to Mrs. Lettice's house.

John Rolfe found nothing amiss with Pocahontas when he saw her the next day, nor did any of the Council members tell him of the falsehood they had related Lady Rebecca. All Rolfe knew was that Pocahontas was responding to him, at last. Indeed, his wooing seemed very gentle and most wonderful to Pocahontas. No Indian lover ever courted his wife in this way, with hand-holding and stolen kisses, with soulful looks and words of love. She listened with amazement when he told her that he wanted her to be his wife and to share a home with him in this new land. When she said yes to him, she felt as if she were the heroine in one of the tales she had heard so often around the fire in the Powhatan village—a deer, perhaps, that was magically transformed into a human shape, or a bird on whom the spirits had bestowed the gift of speech—so happy was John Rolfe with her reply.

A few weeks after she had said yes, the governor, Sir Thomas Dale, had begun to grow impatient for peace with Chief Powhatan. He decided to journey to Werowocomoco taking Pocahontas with him to act as intermediary. Perhaps seeing his daughter would soften Powhatan's defiance. They sailed upriver on Argall's ship, with John Rolfe and one hundred fifty other men.

But when they tried to land at a small village near Werowocomoco, the Indians refused to let them dock. In retaliation, the English fired on them, and so terrified the Indians that they ran off into the forest to escape the white men's weapons. But the colonists went even further: they burned the small lodges and spoiled the corn the Indians had stored away for later use.

Pocahontas felt heartsick at the animosity between the two peoples she loved. She begged Sir Thomas to let her go among her people. "They will listen to me and I can go to my father," she said. "I know that when he actually sees me, he will deny me nothing." Pocahontas paused here, filled with emotion. "And it is so long since I have looked upon his face," she pleaded.

But Sir Thomas refused. He did not want to lose his valuable hostage. Even though Pocahontas might wish to return to the English of her own accord, he was sure Chief Powhatan would try to stop her and would never let her leave his side again.

Pocahontas sighed. "All right, then," she suggested sadly, "at least send messengers in my name, saying that you will refrain from fighting for a night and a day until you can speak face-to-face. Here," she said, plucking a white eagle feather from her headband. "If the messengers take this feather, they will be able to walk in safety."

As the messengers were leaving, she cried out, "And beg of my father to send my brothers to see me, since I cannot go to them."

Now that she was once again so near home, Pocahontas was homesick for her family, her brothers and sisters and cousins whom she had not seen in many moons. She was sure her father would not come because he would not wish to deal with the white men in person. But perhaps she could see Nautauquas or Cleopatra.

Pocahontas waited anxiously, her eyes and ears straining for signs of the returning messengers.

An hour or so later, she saw two tall figures approaching in the distance. She sprang ashore from the boat, her arms outstretched, crying, "Nautauquas! Catanaugh!" as her two brothers hurried to meet her.

"Is it indeed our little Matoaka," asked Nautauquas, "unharmed and well?"

He looked at her carefully, as if seeking to discover some great change in her. "We feared they might have used evil medicine against you, little Snow Feather. Are you truly all right? How have they treated you?"

"Do not be afraid," cried her young brother, Catanaugh, whose glance was fixed upon the paleface's boat. "We shall rescue you if we have to kill every single one of them yonder to free you."

"No, my brothers," said Pocahontas, laying her hand gently on Nautauquas's strong arm. "They are my friends, and they have treated me well. Look! Am I wasted with starvation or broken from torture? Do not harm them, please. I have come to plead with our father to make peace with them. I am like a tree, pleading with the sky and the earth not to quarrel, since both are dear to the tree. The English are a great nation. Let us be friends with them."

"Have they bewitched you, Matoaka?" asked Catanaugh sternly. "Have you forgotten your father's people now that you have dwelt among these strangers?"

"No, brother, but . . ."

Nautauquas was quick to notice Pocahontas's confusion and the blush that stole over her soft dark cheek.

"I think," he said, smiling at her with understanding, "that our little sister has a story to tell us. Let us sit here beneath the trees, as we so often sat in the past, and listen to her words."

It was not easy at first for Pocahontas to explain how she felt about the English and, in particular, about John Rolfe. But as she sat on the warm brown pine needles, snuggled closely against Nautauquas's shoulder, she found the courage to tell both her brothers about the strong, fine Englishman who had taught her so much. "He has asked me to be his wife, my brothers, and to live with him among the white people as a Christian."

The brothers stared at their little sister, shocked by her words.

"And I am already a Christian, my brothers," Pocahontas admitted, her eyes downcast. "My father did not come to my aid and, to be fair, the English were very kind to me. Their god is my god now."

Nautauquas and Catanaugh shook their heads in dismay. Their sister had changed in many ways. It seemed that they did not know her anymore.

Ignoring their reactions, Pocahontas continued. "Sir Thomas Dale, the governor of Jamestown, has given his consent to my marriage to John Rolfe and, in truth, we do care for each other, in even the Indian way of love."

Catanaugh said nothing, but Nautauquas laid his hand on his sister's arm and looked searchingly in her eyes, "Are you happy?" he asked her.

"Yes, brother, very happy. He is dear to me because I know him —and because there is still so much for me to discover. You surely have not forgotten how I have always longed to learn new things and to find new adventures beyond our forest."

"Has Okee given you a sign?" asked Nautauquas.

"Remember, the god of the Christians is my god now," she answered calmly.

Nautauquas nodded again, but Catanaugh scowled. "A woman and a man should worship the same spirits," Nautauquas reprimanded him gently. Then, after a pause, he continued. "So . . . then. All is well with you?"

"All will be well if my father makes peace. It is truly one of the reasons I have consented to this marriage. It is a promise I had given many moons ago to one no longer here. But I gave my word then that I would preserve peace in this land if I could." Pocahontas was silent for a long moment. She sighed deeply, remembering her white brother, John Smith. Then, tapping her hands on her knees, she became herself once more. "So! I very much want to see my father. Does he love me still?" she asked wistfully.

"Our father says he loves you as he loves his own life," Nautauquas answered. "And, though he has many children who delight him, he does not care for any as much as he does for you."

Pocahontas sighed half sadly, half happily. "Give him my love, Brothers," she said, "and say to him that Matoaka's thoughts go out to him each day, just as the tide comes up the river from the sea." The brothers nodded in unison. Catanaugh sifted the brown pine needles through his fingers. He looked intently at his sister and said, "He has agreed to a truce until *taquitock*, autumn, if the English send some important hostages to him whom he can hold as they hold you."

Pocahontas ignored the import of Catanaugh's words. Instead, she thought about the people she loved and missed in Werowocomoco.

"And Cleopatra and our other sisters and old Wansutis, how is it with them," she asked, "and all the others?" Pocahontas listened to all the news her brothers had to tell her of the great

"I do," she answered, looking down.
Page 185

"I thank thee for coming," the queen said graciously.
Page 205

deeds of the young braves, of the wise speeches made by the old chiefs in council, of the harvest dances, of the sad losses on the warpaths, and of old Wansutis, who had grown stranger and more silent since Claw-of-the-Eagle's death.

It was then Pocahontas's turn to tell her brothers how Claw-of-the-Eagle had died. There were tears in their eyes when they heard about the bravery of their adopted brother. Catanaugh's eyes flashed in triumph when he heard about the three palefaces his friend had slain.

The three were so engrossed in their conversation that they did not notice the sun was beginning to set. A breeze came up and the sky turned overcast. They did not realize how long they had been sitting there chatting, until they saw Sir Thomas coming towards them, accompanied by Rolfe and another colonist, Mister Sparkes.

Sir Thomas bowed to Pocahontas. "Here you are! Hello, Princess. We have been looking for you." He pointed to Rolfe and Sparkes. "These two, Princess," he said, "will be the hostages we send to your father." He paused. "We would like the two of you," and he nodded to Pocahontas's brothers, "to stay with us."

The two Indians looked keenly at the white men. From the glance their sister gave Rolfe, they knew he must be her intended husband. Rolfe and his future brothers-in-law gazed at each other with the same curiosity. Rolfe noticed that Pocahontas's brothers were tall like their father, strong and well built. Nautauquas and Rolfe felt an immediate rapport. Rolfe recalled that John Smith had said of Nautauquas that he was "the manliest, most comely, and boldest spirit I had ever seen."

Soon the entire group headed back to Jamestown, except for Rolfe and Sparkes, who continued on to Werowocomoco. They did not fear that harm would come to them, but they sorely begrudged the time that they would spend away from the colony.

Their reception at Werowocomoco was less than cordial. Chief Powhatan, who was still angry with the English, refused to see them, but his brother, Opechancanough, entertained them and promised to intercede on their behalf with his brother. He had already learned that Rolfe was to marry his niece.

The truce remained in effect as autumn became winter. Nautauquas and Catanaugh enjoyed their time on the island among the palefaces—Catanaugh was fascinated by the fort and its guns, and by the ship, as was Nautauquas, who was also very interested in the colonists themselves. The two brothers kept their word: they did not leave Jamestown until Chief Powhatan allowed Rolfe and Sparkes to return home.

The two braves had greatly enjoyed hunting and talking with Pocahontas again. They bade her a tearful good-bye and set off to rejoin their tribe at Werowocomoco the very day that Rolfe and Sparkes returned to Jamestown.

CHAPTER 20

THE WEDDING

Winter turned into spring and the snow melted in great rivulets that ran into the Chesapeake Bay. Furs and hats came off and everyone, Indians and English alike, basked in the early, though weak, sun.

Early one April morning in 1614, all the colonists were astir, men, women, and children alike. Several of the men and some of children had gone into the woods to cut large sprays of wild azalea and magnolia. They were planning to decorate the church with flowers. And a breakfast feast was to be served at the governor's house, a bountiful meal of meat, potatoes, corn, and ale, in celebration of the wedding of Lady Rebecca and Sir John Rolfe.

The men donned their best outfits, sighing at the moth holes in their precious cloth vests and the tears in their Flemish lace collars and cuffs, but satisfied on the whole with their distinguished appearances. The few women of the colony—Mrs. Lettice, Mistress Easton, Elizabeth Parsons, Anne Burroughs, and

179

others—enjoyed dressing themselves in the finery they had packed with such care and misgiving back in England. They looked beautiful in their pale blue and yellow bows, their green sateen gowns and their pink and black lace.

The excitement was contagious. This was, after all, an occasion that no one in the New World had ever witnessed. An English gentleman of distinguished lineage was about to wed the daughter of a great Indian ruler, one in whose power it lay to help or hinder the progress of the first permanent English colony in the New World.

Soon all was ready and the wedding guests began to arrive. The guards at the fort were kept busy welcoming the Indians and diplomatically requesting that they lay aside bows, tomahawks, and knives they carried with them everywhere. Happily, though, it was a day without hostility, as Chief Powhatan had finally consented to his daughter's marriage and this had put an end to the enmity between the two peoples.

Chief Powhatan himself would not come to the ceremony, however; he refused to set foot on any land other than his own. But he had sent Opechancanough, Pocahontas's uncle, as his representative, bearing many messages of affection to "his dearest daughter." The elderly Opechancanough was dressed in the splendid ceremonial garments of his tribe: a feather headdress, leggings, a soft belt, and a long deerskin cloak heavily embroidered with shell beads. Pocahontas's brothers, Nautauquas and Catanaugh, accompanied him. The two wandered as they pleased through the town, but Nautauquas, on seeing John Rolfe arrive in his boat from Varina, his tobacco plantation upstream, left his brother to greet him. His love for Pocahontas made him want to know her future husband better, and he also wanted to hear about the house Rolfe had built for his wife at Varina.

Rolfe, recognizing Nautauquas as he approached, heartily

shook hands and talked with him for a while, inquiring about his family, the harvests, and the people he had known briefly when he was held hostage at Werowocomoco.

After they talked, Rolfe left to visit with the governor and Nautauquas went in search of his brother, but he could not find any sign of him.

Nautauquas's younger brother did not have any interest in Rolfe, a white man he considered to be an enemy. He had strolled toward Pocahontas's house while Nautauquas talked to Rolfe, hoping to speak with his sister in private. He found Pocahontas in a beautiful white buckskin gown, with brightly embroidered moccasins on her feet, and a circlet of beads and shimmering feathers around her head.

"You are not going to wear the white man's clothes for your wedding?" Catanaugh asked, surprised by his sister's traditional Indian dress.

"No, Brother," she answered. "It may be that I shall wear their strange costumes someday and their bright necklaces and jewels when I am officially the wife of an Englishman. But today, I am still the daughter of Powhatan, a brave and powerful Indian chief."

Catanaugh said nothing further. He stood silently in the doorway.

"Enter," invited Pocahontas, "and see how I live."

"I see enough," he answered, turning his head from side to side. He paused. "But where does the white man's Okee live?"

"The god of the Christians?" she asked, puzzled at his question. "Why, he lives everywhere, in the sky above and in the earth around us."

"But where do the medicine men pray to him?" he continued.

"Yonder, in the church, that building with the peak on it," Pocahontas answered, pointing to it from the doorway.

Catanaugh nodded. "I will walk some more," he announced, and then left. When he thought Pocahontas was no longer watching him, he ran in the direction of the church. During his short stay in Jamestown a few months before, he had never been inside the building; he had thought it to be some kind of storehouse.

He found the door open and entered quietly, glancing cautiously around until he had assured himself that it was empty. Then he pushed the door shut and fastened it with the bolt. This done he set about examining the building, slowly and privately. At the opposite end of the doorway, in the direction of the rising sun, was an elevation of three steps which made him think of the raised dais that ran across the end of Powhatan's ceremonial lodge. It was lined with red cedar wood. On it stood a dark wooden table covered with a white cloth, and the sun shining through the windows above made the flower-filled vases that stood upon it glisten brightly. In the center of the church, where Catanaugh stood, there were benches and chairs, arranged in straight rows. And everywhere, wherever it was possible to stand or hang them, was a profusion of fragrant flowering branches and candles waiting to be lit.

The very simplicity of the church awed him. His impulse was to flee out into the sunshine, and he turned toward the door. Then he remembered the reason he had come in the first place, and he stood completely still in the center of the church.

He listened intently, but there was no sound. When he was certain that he was still alone, he took a lump of deer fat from the pouch that hung at his side and smeared it on the sides of the benches and the backs of the chairs. Then, taking a handful of tobacco from the same pouch, he sprinkled a small circle of the weed in the center aisle of the church. When he was finished, Catanaugh seated himself crosslegged inside the circle. Slowly and deliberately, he drew a mask and a gourd rattle filled with pebbles from a larger pouch hidden inside his cloak. He put the mask on his face as carefully as if he were being watched by all his tribe, and he laid the rattle across his knees. Catanaugh was so quiet during all these preparations that anyone who might have been in the church would not have noticed the Indian's presence by sound alone.

Catanaugh had a plan: he had not come to Jamestown merely to witness his sister's wedding; he had decided to conduct a dangerous experiment. Catanaugh was by no means a coward, but, unlike his brother Nautauquas, he was one who followed where others led, who obeyed when others commanded. But now, for the first time in his life, he showed a singular courage, born of hate of the white interlopers, the palefaces who he believed would never become valuable allies and friends. He would gladly have killed them all, and he had grown more and more unhappy at the thought that Pocahontas would join herself to one of them. He knew that her marriage would create a bond of peace between the two people that would make it almost impossible for him, and those who shared his belief, to destroy the white invaders. By performing the ancient Indian ritual in the church, Catanaugh hoped to discover that Pocahontas was being forced into this marriage—in which case he was prepared to rescue her and carry her off at the last moment. But his vision showed him a happy bride, a contented and spiritual young woman very much in love. She would never follow him willingly or go quietly if he tried to force her.

He stood up in the circle of sacred tobacco and tried again to delve into the mind and soul of his sister. He wondered how the white man's strange Okee would answer his call, for he knew he must answer. The incantation was such strong medicine that no spirit could resist it, especially when he shook the sacred rattle,

raising his feet higher and higher, then bending over, then spring-
ing back, round and round on the tips of his toes, always within
the boundary of the tobacco circle.

He had been shaking the rattle gently for fear it might be heard
outside the church. But now, anxious to bring this dreadful task
to an end, he began to shake it with all his might in one last
challenge to the strange spirit.

Bim! Bam! Boom! BOOM! Bim!

Catanaugh jumped like a deer that hears the crackle of a twig
behind it. For the marriage bells had begun to ring out in the
belfry above, and in the deep brazen voice of the bells he thought
he heard the answer his incantation had forced from the white
man's Okee. But the voice was so terrible, so loud, that, forgetting everything he had ever learned from the great medicine men,
forgetting everything but his need to escape, he rushed to the
door, frantically unbolted it and ran, still pursued by the sound
until he reached the fort, where the frightened sentries who had
no orders to keep any Indian from *leaving* the town, let the
masked figure out through the gates.

Reverend James Buck, who with the Reverend Whitaker, was to
perform the ceremony, arrived at the church just as the wedding
party arrived from the other end of the town. As the bells continued to ring he entered the church and his foot hit something
lying on the floor. He stooped and picked up a rattle; his fingers
were covered with brown dust. Hastily seizing a broom which
stood in the vestry room, he swept the tobacco from the aisle and
into a corner. He hid the curious rattle with the broom; there
would be time enough to investigate this later. Then he took his
stand at the altar, where Reverend Whitaker soon joined him,
and the two clergymen watched through the open door as their
flock approached. Most of the congregation was composed of
men, courtly cavaliers in fine—if somewhat faded—garments,

who were dressed as if they were about to enter Westminster Abbey to witness the marriage of a king and queen. Here, too, came the soldiers in leather vests, and the bakers, masons, and carpenters with freshly washed faces and hands, in their Sunday garments of leather and starched white aprons. The few women were as colorful as peacocks in their bright taffeta and lace, which today took the place of their workaday blacks and browns.

When the congregation had filled every seat and the overflow had lined up against the walls, a number of Indians, all relatives of Pocahontas, slipped in and stood silently, their eyes keen and curious in their solemn faces. The candles in the aisles had been lit, adding a romantic touch to the simple church.

Finally, with the bells still ringing, Pocahontas entered the church escorted by Opechancanough and Nautauquas.

Pocahontas looked radiant in her white robe and turquoise beads. Her dark hair shone in a gleaming braid. On her wrists she wore bracelets of shell, coral, and turquoise. She wore a long white veil made of lace she had tatted herself.

A sudden feeling of the wonder of this marriage overcame Alexander Whitaker. This Indian maiden, a creature of the woods, shy and proud as a wild animal, was to be married by him to an Englishman with centuries of Western civilization behind him. What did it mean for them both and for their peoples?

Then, with love for the maiden whom he had baptized, and with faith in his heart, he listened while Reverend Buck conducted the ceremony, until it was time for him to ask in a loud, clear voice, "Rebecca, will you take this man to be thy wedded husband?"

"I do," she answered looking down.

"John Rolfe, do you take this woman to be your wedded wife?"

"I do," he said, staring longingly at his Indian bride.

The bells began to ring anew. As the crowd cheered, John Rolfe raised Pocahontas's veil and gently kissed her. Then they walked out of the church hand in hand.

After a feast of venison, pheasant, turkey, and exotic fruits and wine, the bride, using her husband's first name for the first time, asked shyly, "John, will you walk with me into the forest for a little while?"

And Rolfe, anxious to escape the noisy crowd, rose immediately to go with her.

"Why did you wish to come here?" he asked his wife when they had walked a distance into the woods, which were flecked with the white of the innumerable dogwood trees.

"Because," she answered, "Jamestown feels too small to me today, John. Because I have always sought the forest when I have been happy or sad. Because it seems to me that the trees and the beasts would be hurt if I did not let them see me on this great day."

"It is a pretty thought, but a pagan one, my love," said Rolfe, frowning slightly.

But Pocahontas did not notice. She had caught a glimpse of a deer through the leafy branches of the trees; she then saw a striped chipmunk peer at her from an branch overhead.

"Hello, little friends," she called out to them gaily. "Here is Pocahontas to greet you. Wish her happiness, that her nest may be filled with nuts, Little Dancing Chipmunk, and cool shade, on hot noondays, Bright-Eyed Deer." Then, as two wood pigeons flew by, she clapped her hands gently together and cried, "Here is *my* mate, Swift Winged Pigeons. Wish us happiness."

And John Rolfe, sober Englishman that he was, felt rise in him a new kinship with all the living, breathing things of the world, and he wondered if this Indian maiden he had made his wife did not know more of the secrets of the earth than even the wisest men of his own civilization.

CHAPTER 21

ON THE TRAIL OF A THIEF

Wearing a beige dress and a plain bonnet tied with a blue bow, Pocahontas was returning home to Varina from Jamestown. She had gone there with her husband and had left him there to attend to some business. The boatmen escorted her from the skiff and doffed their hats in respect as she delicately pulled up her skirts to avoid the water on the plantation dock.

Two years had already passed since Pocahontas had married John Rolfe and had adopted English ways. In those two years, the young Indian maiden had learned many things: to speak fluently the language of her husband's people, to wear corsets and the formal dress of her new countrywomen in public, and to behave in the manner expected of the English noble class. She had always been accustomed to the deference paid her as the daughter of a great chieftain and ruler of more than thirty tribes, and now she also received the same respect from the English, who treated her like the daughter of a powerful ally. For Chief Powhatan had seen the wisdom of keeping peace between Werowocomoco and Jamestown as well as with the newer settlements that had sprung up along the river, including Rolfe's estate, Varina.

Indeed, so stately was the manner of the Lady Rebecca that it was difficult for people to recall the wide-eyed girl who at one time came and went at Jamestown with such swiftness and quicksilver energy.

Now, as she ascended the hill toward the plantation, Pocahontas's eyes rested on the home Rolfe had built for her. To an Englishman, accustomed to the spacious manor houses of his homeland, Varina appeared to be little more than a cabin. But to one who had seen nothing finer than the skin-and-wood lodges of Werowocomoco, it was a very grand structure indeed, solidly framed in oak, boasting a brick chimney and four brightly painted rooms, fitted out with delicate, embroidered furnishings sent over from London. Rolfe had promised Pocahontas that they would bring back many other wonderful things when they visited England in a few months' time.

Pocahontas was a little flushed from her climb up the hill to Varina and she was looking forward to discarding her clothes in favor of the loose buckskin robe and moccasins she wore when she was alone. Even though he had never spoken a word of criticism to her, Pocahontas knew her husband disapproved of her Indian garb; she was secretly relieved that he would be absent for several days, so she could forget to be a proper English lady.

But she could never forget that she was a mother, that her wonderful little Thomas, neither as white as his father, nor as dark as herself, was waiting for her at the house. She hurried on, thinking of the fun she would have with him—how she would take him down to the stream and let him lie naked on the warm rocks, how she would sing Indian songs to him and tell him stories of the beasts of the woods, even if he was too little to understand what she was telling him.

She had left him in his cradle where, protected by its high sides, he was safe for hours at a time. The workmen who were helping her husband with his tobacco crop had promised to look in often to make sure he was all right.

Pocahontas entered the house and hurried to the cradle, calling out, "Here I am, Little Rabbit."

But when she bent over the side she saw that the cradle was empty!

She searched every room, but found no sign of her son, and then rushed to the door, shouting. Three of the workmen came running and, speaking all at once, they explained to her that, about half an hour after she and Master Rolfe had left, one of them had gone to look in on Thomas and had found the cradle empty. Since then, they had been searching all over Varina, with no success.

It was impossible for Thomas to have left the cradle or the house by himself, but who would have taken him away? Either Indian or white, there was none in all Virginia who would dare to injure the grandchild of Chief Powhatan.

After she had heard what the workmen had to say, Pocahontas told them to continue their search. When they had left, she sat down, not on the wide chair a carpenter had made her as a wedding gift, but on the floor—in the manner that she had so often sat around her father's lodge fire when she wished to think long and hard.

After a time of absolute silence and meditation, Pocahontas rose. She ripped off her bonnet, gown, and her shoes, and dressed in her Indian garments. With each change of clothing, she became more and more her old self, more and more attuned to the secrets and subtleties of the natural world around her.

She knelt by the cradle and examined the floor carefully, then she looked closely at the doorway and the ground in front of it. She sniffed the air eagerly like a hound that had found a scent. Werowocomoco—that was where she must go.

She turned and started in the direction of the village, bending down every few minutes to examine the ground, intent on her quest.

Her first clue was the faint imprint of a moccasined foot. Her brothers and sisters came to see her occasionally, but why, she wondered, would one of them steal her child? And there were no longer any hostile Indians in the region, thanks to their fear of Chief Powhatan's might and the English guns.

But only Indians wore moccasins, and only Indians left the lightest touch on the earth when they moved. The Indian she was following might or might not have her Thomas—and so she thought, until she found a piece of the shell necklace she had made and placed around her baby's neck, flung carelessly aside and half hidden by a rock.

Who could the mysterious Indian kidnapper be?

Once Pocahontas had found the trail, it did not enter her mind to return to the workmen for help or to send a messenger to Jamestown to fetch her husband. She knew beyond all doubt that she was far more able than any white man to swiftly and surely follow in the direction her child had gone. Since the thief had several hours' advantage, it could be days before she caught up with them. But even if it took years and she had to journey to the end of the world she would neither falter nor turn back for help.

As she traveled through the forest in a quick step that was nearly a trot, the polish of her English life fell away from her as the leaves fell from the trees above her head. Pocahontas forgot the events of the two years since she had become Lady Rebecca. She forgot her husband. Her baby was no longer the Rolfe heir, soon to be taken on a journey across the sea to be shown to his kinsmen. No, Thomas was now her Indian child, and as she ran, she called out to him all the pet names that Indian mothers use for their babies. When she thought that he might be crying with terror or hunger, she began to pray, prayers that came from deep in her heart, prayers that were not addressed to the Christian God, but to Okee, the Great Spirit her ancestors had worshipped and her Indian people worshipped still.

Often the trail was almost invisible; there was never a true, direct path. But Pocahontas's eyes, still as keen as they had been when she was younger, were able to keep up. Everything held a clue: pebbles that had been displaced on the ground, the bushes from which raindrops had been shaken, a broken twig—all helped her read the way she was to go. If she could only tell whether she might be gaining on them!

What she would do when she came face-to-face with the kidnapper, Pocahontas did not know. If he were a strong man who defied her command to give up the grandson of Chief Powhatan, how could she make him do so? She had started off so hastily that she had not armed herself with any weapon. But she did not doubt that, in one way or another, she would get her child back.

The sun was sinking; its rays struck the lower parts of the tree trunks. Seeing this, Pocahontas ran faster. Once night fell, she would have to lie down and wait for morning for fear of missing a clue and losing the trail.

It was almost dark when she reached open space, a meadow where wild animals came to drink from a spring that bubbled up in its center by a growth of young trees. On one side of the ground, covered with moss and creeping crowfoot, there were overhanging rocks which formed a small cave not much deeper than a man's height.

Since she could no longer see any footprints in the gathering dusk, Pocahontas sadly prepared to spend the long night in this shelter. She leaned down and drank deeply from the spring. Taking off her moccasins, she bathed her tired feet in it. Then, because she wanted a fire, more for companionship than for warmth, she gathered some twigs. Twirling one in a bit of rotten wood, she soon produced a spark that lighted a cheerful blaze.

There was nothing to be gained by staying awake. There was no one from whom she had anything to fear except the kidnapper—and the sooner they met the better she would feel. With the disappearance of her child she had lost everything, and she was no longer afraid of anything.

The warmth of the fire made Pocahontas feel drowsy; she was bone tired from her long pursuit. She lay down at the entrance of the cave, half in and half out, and, in a moment, was fast asleep.

Several times during the night, she was half awakened by the sound of some young animal crying—perhaps a bear cub, she thought sleepily, but even if the mother bear was nearby, Pocahontas felt no fear.

Later, she dreamed that the mother bear had come into the cave and was sniffing her all over. She opened her eyes and saw the glow from the fire's embers reflected in a pair of eyes above her.

"Go away, old Furry One!" Pocahontas commanded drowsily. "I am not afraid of you. Leave me and let me sleep."

But the sound of her own voice awakened her fully and she raised herself to a sitting position to see if the bear was indeed obeying her. Against the almost extinguished embers, Pocahontas saw the dim outline, not of the expected mother bear, but of a human being! She sprang up, seized hold of a limb with her right hand before the person had time to escape, and, with her left hand, snatched up some dried twigs and threw them on the remains of the fire. The wood, already heated, ignited at once. The blaze lighted up the little forest cave and Pocahontas beheld old Wansutis!

"Where is my child?" cried Pocahontas. "What have you done with him?" She shook the old woman in fury and in fear. "Only you would dare steal him from me! What have you done with him? Where is he? Speak!"

The old woman did not struggle in Pocahontas's firm grasp. She stood still, as if alone, staring into the flames that reddened the trees outside the cave as if they were stained with blood.

"What have you done with my son?" Pocahontas screamed again.

"What have you done with *my* son?" Wansutis shouted back, without turning her head from the blazing fire.

"*Your* son? Claw-of-the-Eagle? What do you mean?" Pocahontas asked. "I sent you word of his death many, many moons ago."

Wansutis continued to stare at the fire. "If you had loved him," she said, slowly and deliberately, "he would not have died."

Pocahontas drew her hand over her face. "I loved him as a sister, Wansutis," she said to the old woman. "But my fate did not lie in his hands or mine. Yes, Claw-of-the-Eagle is dead, and we mourn him, you and I," and here she loosened her grasp on the old woman's shoulder, "but my son is *alive*." Pocahontas paused. "Unless—" she gasped, unable to continue. The dreadful possibility of Wansutis's vengeance made her shake like leaves in the wind.

She began to cry. Her hands fluttered helplessly. "What have you done with my son, Wansutis?" Pocahontas asked quietly. "What did you want with him?"

Wansutis crouched down, looking at the heart of the fire. She began to chant, as if alone. "Wansutis's son died in battle. There was no stronger, fiercer brave in all the thirty tribes, and Wansutis's lodge was empty and there was no one to hunt for her.

Then Wansutis saw a prisoner with a strong, young body, though he was still small, and, right then, Wansutis had a new son! A new boy to love, a swift hunter whose face was ruddy in the firelight, whose presence in her lodge made Wansutis's sleep quiet. But," she continued chanting, "but this son wanted a maiden for his wife and he went forth to play his music and woo her. The maiden would not listen, and so the river and the maiden killed the brave second son of Wansutis, and once again her lodge is lonely."

She stopped for a moment, then, as if she were reading the words in the flames. She sang more slowly. "I am old, old Wansutis, yet I will live for many harvests. I have another son now. I will take him to my wigwam. He shall watch me and protect me. He will cheer me in the winters and I will love him with all my heart."

Pocahontas's face blazed with fury. Her eyes darkened. "So that is the reason you stole my child! You cannot keep him! He is mine, not yours. He will go with his father and with his mother to grow up in England." Her voice rose in defiance. "He is my son, my son whom I love more than life itself."

Suddenly, a cry came from the woods, the same cry Pocahontas had heard in her dreams. Without a moment's hesitation, the young woman sprang into the blackness and, in a few minutes, she returned with her baby in her arms. She squatted down by the fire and touched him all over, clasping him to her breast, rocking him and singing until she was convinced that he was unharmed.

Wansutis rose. "Farewell, Princess," she said. "Wansutis will now return to her lodge alone."

Now that she had her child safely in her arms, Pocahontas's kind heart began to speak. "Wansutis, you know I cannot let you have my Thomas, but I will ask my father to give you the very next young brave he captures so you will no longer be lonely."

Wansutis shook her head. "I will seek no more sons," she answered. "Perhaps he would set off for a faraway land and leave me even as you, your father's daughter, leave him."

"But I will return," Pocahontas protested.

"Do you know that?" the old woman asked, leaning down and peering directly into Pocahontas's face. Her gaze was so full of hatred that Pocahontas drew back in terror.

Wansutis grinned with evil knowledge. "I see a ship," she began to chant. "I see a ship that sails for many days toward the rising sun, but I never see the ship that sails to the sunset. I see a deer from the free forests and it is fettered and its neck is hung with beads and flowers. The deer seeks in vain to escape from its bed of ferns in the woodlands, but it cannot." Wansutis spread her arms, and stared into the flames. "I see a bird that is caught where the lodges are closer together than the pebbles on a seashore. But I never see the bird fly free above the tops of the lodges." She crossed her arms over the flames. "I see an orphan child. He is crying, but his mother lies still. She cannot hear him."

Pocahontas held Thomas tightly. She gazed in horrible fascination at the old woman who, with another harsh laugh, vanished into the darkness.

CHAPTER 22

POCAHONTAS IN ENGLAND

Pocahontas was happy and excited on the day she set sail for England with her husband and child. They were accompanied by Sir Thomas Dale, the governor, and by Chief Uttamatomakkin, an elder chief whom Powhatan had sent as his representative, and who was to observe the English and their ways in their own land.

Pocahontas was going to England! She could not believe it. Everything about the voyage interested her: the ship itself, the hoisting and furling of the sails, the storminess of the lapping waves, the songs the sailors sang as they worked, the sight of spouting whales, and, as they neared the English coast, a magnificent warship which was, the captain declared, a veteran of the battle against the Spanish Armada.

During the long, starlit evenings, Rolfe told Pocahontas wonderful stories from English history. He recounted tales of heroes and recited lovely, romantic poems.

But for Pocahontas, the most fascinating aspect of the journey was the unchanging ocean, the vast body of water so unlike the forest, on which no tracks could be seen, an azure sea that was somehow connected to other lands—and which could be traveled by people who knew how to guide themselves by the stars! It was a marvel to her that men were able to sail ships back and forth across it. Although she heard many explanations of how this was done, none lessened her amazement. To Pocahontas, it was this ability to travel the sea that most exemplified the white man's ingenuity.

One day, a gray cloud could be seen on the eastern horizon. A seagull squawked overhead. John Rolfe's face changed as he stared at the grayness in the distance.

"England!" he cried. He lifted little Thomas to his shoulder and pointed. "Look! There is your father's home!"

When the ship dropped anchor at Plymouth, curious and excited officers from the Virginia Company came to greet Pocahontas, the daughter of an Indian ally, the extent of whose power they could only imagine. They had arranged suitable lodgings for Lady Rebecca and her family in London and, with much bowing and waving of plumed hats, they promised to grant her every wish.

These men were different from any Pocahontas had ever met. The colonists were so energetic, hardworking, and adventurous. These men seemed, in contrast, so comfortable and self-satisfied. They were a new kind of white men, as different to her as she was to them.

During the bumpy carriage ride to London, Pocahontas asked question after question, exclaiming in interest and delight about the cottages they passed; the beautiful trimmed hedges; the lush, green farms; and the meadows where cattle and horses grazed behind carefully constructed fences.

When they stopped at an inn for the night, Pocahontas did not go straight to bed. Instead, she was eager to examine everything, from the opulent sitting rooms to the fragrant attics where bunches of herbs hung from the rafters. But despite her girlish excitement, Pocahontas bore herself with such dignity that no one could have even a single doubt that she was a woman of high birth.

"Ah, John!" she sighed one day, as the carriage gently carried them past a blooming apple orchard. "This is so fair a land. I do not understand how you ever left it. At night, when I go to sleep, I can scarcely wait for morning to come. There is always something new to discover—and you know how my spirit loves new things."

Rolfe smiled. He covered his wife's gloved hand with his own. "As does mine, Rebecca. It is for that reason that I traveled to the New World—and why I rejoiced in its strangeness, just as you rejoice in the strange, new things in my land."

The nearer they got to London, the more there was to see. The highway was soon filled with those coming and going from town: merchants with their carts jangling with goods, farmers with their produce, butchers with squawking chickens and slow-moving cattle, traveling jugglers and actors, peddlers selling medicines and magic, colorful gypsies, great ladies and men on horseback or in coaches, who stared at Pocahontas and whispered among themselves. Pocahontas asked Rolfe about each and every individual she saw, who they were and where they lived.

When they reached the outskirts of London, the crowds increased. Pocahontas turned to Rolfe and asked, "Is a war party returning from a victory? Or are you celebrating a festival day?"

Rolfe smiled again and explained that London was like this every single day. She could hardly believe it. People pushed through the crowds to stare at Pocahontas—and at Uttamato-makkin in his traditional Indian dress. The crowds of curious

"Perhaps someday you will take me to your father's court," she said, "but in the meantime I have come to take you to the court of our queen. She has expressed the desire to see you." Lady De La Ware paused, cooling her face with an elaborately painted fan. "A letter that Captain John Smith wrote to her about you made her very curious, and very much eager to honor the brave young woman who saved our colony."

Pocahontas stared at her new friend. "Captain John Smith wrote to the Queen about me?"

"Indeed, he did." Lady De La Ware told Pocahontas how Smith had written of his rescue in Chief Powhatan's lodge, of the journeys Pocahontas had made to save Jamestown's colonists from dying of starvation, and of her intervention when Smith and his party were almost ambushed by an angry, betrayed Chief Powhatan.

Pocahontas assumed that Smith had written all this from Jamestown, before his death. She was overwhelmed when she realized that even as he lay dying she was in his thoughts, that he wanted to honor her.

The truth, as Lady De La Ware and the rest of the guests knew, was that Captain John Smith was very much alive and well. Indeed, he was in Plymouth, making ready to start another expedition to New England. Although he did not expect to see Pocahontas, he had recently written to his queen about her. He wanted everyone in England to know what they owed this young Indian woman.

Not long after the ball, Pocahontas herself discovered the truth. She and Rolfe were visiting a family in the country; she was walking through a garden of roses and lilacs and peonies with a young woman called Miss Alicia, who pleaded with Pocahontas to take her to the New World when she returned. She wanted to see the Indians for herself.

Pocahontas was only half listening to the girl's chatter. She was thinking about the past. Ever since her conversation with Lady De La Ware, she could not get John Smith out of her mind.

Suddenly, Alicia stopped talking and gestured to two men walking down the garden path toward them. "Look," she said, "here comes your husband and, oh yes, silly me, it is Captain John Smith. Of course he would come to see you. I want to stay and hear what you two old friends say to each other after all this time!" Alicia clapped her white-gloved hands in excitement, almost dropping her pale blue parasol in the process.

It seemed to Pocahontas that hours instead of minutes elapsed as the men approached. How could Smith be alive when she knew that he was dead? But as she heard his voice, as she saw his face, she knew, with all her heart, that it was her brother. And she remembered that the only word she had heard about his death had come from councilmen who had had their own reasons for lying.

Pocahontas thought she might faint as Rolfe came forward with Smith. Luckily, a bee buzzed by, startling her and helping her to regain her composure.

"I have brought you an old friend, Rebecca," Rolfe said.

Pocahontas smiled. Words were impossible. She turned away for fear of betraying her emotions and hid her face behind a fan. The men, assuming that she wanted to be alone, left with Miss Alicia to take some tea on the terrace.

She sighed deeply as they walked away. Quietly, almost in slow motion, she sat down on a stone garden bench near a fish pond. Her life, the time she had spent with John Smith, his face, his voice, the touch of his hand—all these memories washed over her.

Then she saw him coming toward her again, alone. Overcome with happiness she reached out her hand to take his. She could no more be angry with Smith than a branch could quarrel with its tree, a flower with its roots. She was just so relieved and happy to see him again.

"My brother!" she cried, "do you remember the old days in the New World when you first came to Werowocomoco and were my prisoner?"

"I remember well, Lady Rebecca," he said, leaning down to kiss her hand, "and I am forever in your debt."

Pocahontas frowned and tossed her dark hair, which hung in curls around her face. "Do not call me by that strange name. I will always be Matoaka to you. Do you remember the night I sneaked through the forest to warn you?"

"I remember, Matoaka," he replied gravely. "How could I ever forget?" Smith's eyes filled with wonder at the woman before him. Pocahontas had grown up; she was no longer the young Indian girl he had known. She was a beautiful, majestic woman. He shook his head, leaving many thoughts unspoken, realizing that their destinies would remain forever unfulfilled.

"Do you remember the day when you were lying wounded before your house and you made me promise to be a friend to Jamestown and the English?" Pocahontas asked.

"I have thought about it often," he replied.

Pocahontas looked up at Smith, her eyes vulnerable. "I have kept my promise, Brother, have I not?"

"Most nobly, Matoaka. And I will never forget. But, please, do not call me brother here. People will not understand."

Pocahontas tossed her head emphatically and this gesture brought back to Smith the bright, young Indian girl who, for a moment, had been disguised by her fashionable English clothes.

"But we made a pact, remember, John Smith? Remember the night you and my father promised to honor each other always, and that our lands and our fates would always be the same?"

"But Princess," Smith sighed, sitting down next to her on the bench. "It is different here. The king would be unhappy if he heard you call me "brother" and I called you "sister." He would think that my enemies spoke the truth: that I wanted more power than I have."

Pocahontas brushed a fly from her face. She grimaced. "What is this I hear from you? You were not afraid to come to my country when you knew it not. You were not afraid to travel across the sea and through the forests. But now, here, in your own land, you are afraid?"

Smith laughed and shook his head. She was right. Pocahontas was always right. "Call me what you will then," he said. "I will fear no evil that could ever come to me from you."

Pocahontas then spoke a few words to him in the Powhatan language, anxious to see if he still remembered it. He did. Pocahontas smiled, but only for a moment. She fell silent.

"What is it, Matoaka? What weary thoughts have crossed your mind?" asked Smith.

Pocahontas bit her lip and told him the truth. "They told me you were dead and I did not know otherwise until this afternoon."

Smith took her hand and looked into her eyes. "Think no more of it, little sister. I am not dead yet and, I promise with all my heart that we will greet each other again. When I return from New England we will spend many days and nights talking about our time together. I promise never again to forsake you."

Pocahontas shook her head. "I shall not remain here long, my brother. We, too, set sail soon. I have been happy in your land, but I am now suffering from an illness they tell me is called homesickness."

"That is an illness which is easily remedied, Matoaka. But

when you return to your land, forget not the country nor the friends who will never forget you."

John Smith kissed her hand and touched her cheek. He bowed. "Until one day soon, my sister." He turned and walked back to the terrace.

The next few weeks passed quickly. There was so much to see and to do. Pocahontas attended a play called *The Tempest*, written by a man named Will Shakespeare, and went to a poetry reading by a wise, witty man called Ben Johnson. There were more balls and more dresses to fit and more dinners to attend. But, always, at the times she least expected it, Pocahontas would think of John Smith.

At last, the day came when she was to be presented to Queen Anne, consort of King James of England. Lady De La Ware helped Pocahontas dress and taught her how to curtsy. As they approached the queen's chambers, there were many halls and anterooms filled with courtiers and ladies, all wearing elaborate white wigs, brilliant satins, and necklaces of precious gems. All of them looked at Pocahontas with envy; it was the greatest honor to be received by the queen.

At long last, they reached the large hall where the queen sat. It was hung with rich tapestries and furnished with dark oak chairs and couches covered with purple velvet. As Pocahontas and Lady De La Ware approached, Queen Anne waved her ladies-in-waiting and her servants away. She curtsied after Pocahontas did. They smiled at each other, but the queen did not stretch out her hand to be kissed—which she would have done had she not considered Pocahontas an equal. Both were of royal blood. Each was the princess of a great land.

"I thank you for coming," the queen said graciously. "I have very much desired to see you. Captain Smith was right when he told me what our people owe you, and he most of all."

"He was kind to my people as well," answered Pocahontas.

The two women settled down on a purple couch and began to talk. They discussed Captain Smith and ocean voyages; they described their children and they chatted with each other about their husbands.

While they sat talking, there was a sudden commotion at the end of the hall. The servants were very excited and uncertain about what they should do. However, the matter was decided for them when Uttamatomakkin, strong and powerful and clad in his long mantle, moccasins, and feathered headdress, strode in. Pocahontas watched him eagerly examine all the furnishings in the hall; she saw his gaze rest on the queen.

"Is this the squaw of the great White Chief?" he asked Pocahontas in their own tongue. "I have already beheld the king and he is a weak little creature whom any child at Werowocomoco could knock down."

"Who is he and what does he say?" asked the queen, who was delighted by his strange appearance.

"This is Uttamatomakkin, one of my people, Madame Queen," Pocahontas replied. With amazing diplomacy, she added, "And he compliments both you and your handsome king."

The queen, whose curiosity was great, beckoned to Uttamatomakkin to come closer. The elder chief fearlessly approached the couch.

"What is this made of?" asked the sovereign, taking up an end of the painted and embroidered deerskin robe and rubbing it critically between her fingers.

Uttamatomakkin, assuming that this was an English form of salutation, caught hold of Queen Anne's green velvet skirt, and to the accompaniment of little shrieks of dismay from her ladies-in-waiting, fingered it in the same manner.

In the Powhatan language Pocahontas told him to stop at once, but Uttamatomakkin merely grunted. "Why should I not do what she has done to me?"

The queen quickly recovered her composure. As a token of goodwill, she unfastened a golden brooch from her vest and pinned it to the Indian's robe. Not to be outdone, Uttamatomakkin took a shell bead from his pouch and fastened it to a pearl pin on the queen's bodice.

"I see I cannot get the better of him, Lady Rebecca," said the queen, laughing. "But ask him what he does with that long stick he carries."

The servants and the ladies-in-waiting had moved closer to the small group by the couch. They stared and listened as Uttamatomakkin took out the stick; it was covered with little nicks. In his own tongue, which Pocahontas translated, he told the queen that Chief Powhatan had told him to mark the stick every time he saw a paleface in this strange land. "But there are so many and the stick is so short," he said. "Chief Powhatan does not realize how the palefaces swarm here like bees in a hollow tree," Uttamatomakkin grumbled.

Pocahontas repeated his words to Queen Anne; she was greatly amused.

"But surely you do not plan to leave soon, Lady Rebecca?" she asked.

Pocahontas shook her head. She rose to go. "As much as I like your land and its people, the time draws near for us to return to my homeland. Farewell, my queen."

Accompanied by Lady De La Ware and Uttamatomakkin, Pocahontas left the audience chamber.

The queen stared after the group. "The Lady Rebecca," she

said to her ladies-in-waiting when the curtains had fallen behind Pocahontas, "is one of the gentlest ladies that England has ever welcomed."

Pocahontas did not yet know that she would never see her beloved Werowocomoco again. Her illness was not homesickness after all, but tuberculosis, of which she died early in the spring of 1617. She was barely twenty-one years old.

It is said that as she lay dying, she faced the window to the west, where the leaves on the trees waved in the wind, where the green forests were illuminated by the brilliant sun high in the blue skies, where the Great Spirits, both Indian and Christian alike, were joined together in peace and harmony.

Outside that window was a world in which Pocahontas, the charismatic girl, the Indian princess, the heroine, the legend, would have been very much at home.